Empowering Strategic Change

Empowering Strategic Change

Conversation-focused Project Leadership

Kathy Cowan Sahadath

BEP

BUSINESS EXPERT PRESS

Leader in applied, concise business books

Empowering Strategic Change:
Conversation-focused Project Leadership

Cover design by Cassandra Kronstedt

Interior design by S4Carlisle Publishing Services, Chennai, India

First published in 2025 by
Business Expert Press, LLC
222 East 46th Street, New York, NY 10017
www.businessexpertpress.com

ISBN-13: 978-1-63742-923-5 (paperback)
ISBN-13: 978-1-63742-924-2 (e-book)

Portfolio and Project Management Collection

First edition: 2025

10 9 8 7 6 5 4 3 2 1

EU SAFETY REPRESENTATIVE
Mare Nostrum Group B.V.
Mauritskade 21D
1091 GC Amsterdam
The Netherlands
gpsr@mare-nostrum.co.uk

Description

In times of complexity and transformation, leadership is no longer just about strategy and execution, it's about conversation. *Empowering Strategic Change: Conversation-focused Project Leadership* offers a compelling new framework that positions dialogue, storytelling, and reflective practice at the heart of effective project and change leadership.

Drawing on the author's research in leadership conversations, adult learning, and systems thinking, as well as years of consulting across industries, this book introduces a **Dual-Lens Framework**, a practical model that helps leaders understand both how their conversations are experienced (Lens 1) and what they are designed to accomplish (Lens 2). Through real-world case studies, accessible tools, and thoughtfully designed reflection exercises, readers learn how to shift from transactional communication to transformational leadership.

The author clearly demonstrates how reflective dialogue and narrative capacity enables leaders to build trust, interpret change, align strategy with purpose, and guide teams through ambiguity. Each chapter integrates practical techniques such as the Conversation Function Audit, Leadership Narrative Playback, and the Dual-Lens Storytelling Checklist, making the book a hands-on resource for project, change, and executive leaders alike.

Whether you're leading a project rollout, a culture shift, or a cross-functional initiative, *Empowering Strategic Change: Conversation-focused Project Leadership* offers the insight and tools to lead with greater clarity, connection, and impact, one conversation at a time.

Contents

List of Figures and Tables

Figures

Tables

Acknowledgments

This book would not have been possible without the support, insight, and encouragement of many people along the way.

To my family, friends, colleagues, and collaborators (past and present), thank you for the engaging conversations, thoughtful feedback, and shared commitment to meaningful leadership. Your contributions helped shape the ideas and tools in these pages. To the leaders and teams I've had the privilege of working with, your courage, curiosity, and honesty in navigating change inspired much of what this book explores. The real-world experiences you shared gave life to theory and grounded every chapter in practice.

To the editorial and publishing team, your guidance, professionalism, and attention to detail brought this vision to life. I'm deeply grateful for your partnership. And to the readers, thank you for investing your time and trust. I hope this book becomes a helpful companion in your leadership journey, sparking reflection, dialogue, and meaningful change.

To my greatest supporters—my late husband and my brilliant son—thank you for always believing in me. Your wisdom, love, and curiosity have shaped how I see the world.

—Kathy

Review Quotes

"Finally! A book that speaks to the real heart of project leadership. Not just schedules and deliverables, but the conversations that build trust, shift thinking, and move teams forward. The tools in this book are immediately usable, but what really stayed with me was how it helped me see my role differently. Can't wait until it's published."—**Senior Project Manager, Tech and Innovation Portfolio**

*"*Empowering Strategic Change *bridges the gap between theory and practice with elegance. As a change consultant, I've seen firsthand how reflective conversation reshapes organizational culture. This book gave me a framework to name what I knew intuitively, and apply it more effectively. Thank you for the opportunity to review this thoughtful and timely work."*—**Organizational Change Advisor**

"In a time when leadership can feel performative or reactive, this book reminds us of something deeper: that transformation begins in dialogue. The Dual-Lens Framework offers a language and discipline for the kind of leadership our teams are craving, empathetic, strategic, and grounded in meaning. I'm grateful to have had the chance to read this in draft form. The insights and practical tools will stay with me long after I turn the last page."—**Executive Vice President, Healthcare Systems Integration**

Introduction:
Why Leadership
Conversations Matter

"Leadership isn't just what you do. It's how you talk while doing it."

In today's fast-paced, complex project environments, success is often defined by outcomes: deadlines met, resources allocated, milestones achieved. But the true test of leadership, especially in times of uncertainty, is not merely execution. It's the ability to shape meaning, spark alignment, and build trust through conversation.

At the heart of every change effort lies a question: What kind of conversations are we having and what kind of leadership are we creating?

This book begins with a simple premise: Strategic leadership lives in conversation. The words we choose, the questions we ask, and the stories we tell define how others experience change. When conversations create clarity, connection, and commitment, change moves from plan to practice. When they don't, even the most sophisticated strategy will stall.

Why Now:
The Urgency of Human-Centered Leadership

Organizations across sectors are navigating sweeping disruption, from digital transformation and equity reform to workforce renewal and systemic redesign. These pressures are not only technical but also deeply human. As complexity rises, so too does the need for leadership that is reflective, adaptive, and empathetic.

Yet traditional models of project and change leadership still rely heavily on control, compliance, and post hoc communication. Leaders are trained to manage tasks and strategies but rarely equipped to facilitate meaning. In response, this book offers a new approach: leadership through intentional, purposeful conversation.

Informed by many years of business practice, original doctoral research, and insights from senior leaders across industries, this book introduces the **Dual-Lens Framework**, a practical model that helps leaders align their inner awareness with the outer purpose of their conversations. It provides a way to lead change with people, not to them, and to make leadership a relational act, not just a functional one.

A Story That Changed My View

Years ago, I was called in to support a large public sector transformation. The project plan was sound. The technical teams were capable. Yet something wasn't working. Resistance was rising. Engagement was falling. Despite early momentum, progress had stalled.

As I listened in on team meetings, a pattern emerged: Conversations were one-way, rushed, and transactional. Updates flowed from the top, but meaning never took root. No space existed for questions, doubts, or dialogue. The change was being implemented but not understood. It wasn't the strategy that was failing; rather, it was the story.

When we finally slowed down to ask, "What does this mean for us?" Everything shifted. People opened up. Teams got curious. Resistance turned into insight. What moved the project forward wasn't a new tool or timeline. It was a new kind of conversation. And with it, a new kind of leadership.

From Communication to Conversation

Many leaders still treat communication as a final step, something to manage once the "real work" is done. But in practice, conversation is the work. It is how we:

- Translate vision into relevance
- Align priorities and expectations
- Surface resistance and wisdom
- Sustain morale and motivation

Especially in complex change, leadership is not about knowing all the answers. It's about creating the conditions for shared sensemaking, where people feel seen, heard, and invited into the journey.

This is not soft leadership. Rather, it's strategic. It's how people make meaning in motion, and how organizations build cultures of purpose and adaptability.

The Research Behind the Framework

In my doctoral research (Sahadath 2010), I set out to understand how senior leaders made sense of their leadership conversations during times of change. Using phenomenography (Akerlind 2025), a qualitative research method that examines variation in experience, I uncovered five distinct ways leaders understood the purpose and value of conversation. Their conversations were:

1. Strategically Intentional—Directing and influencing action
2. Catalyst for Change—Sparking new insights and possibilities
3. Mindful Awareness—Cocreating meaning in real time
4. Building Shared Commitment—Deepening trust and engagement
5. Guiding the Change—Leading systemwide transformation

These are not fixed styles. They are developmental perspectives. Each one represents a way of being in conversation and a pathway to deeper leadership impact.

To make this research actionable, I developed the **Dual-Lens Framework**, which integrates Lens 1: How leaders experience conversation (phenomenographic categories) with Lens 2: What conversations are designed to accomplish (functional types).

This framework gives leaders both a mirror and a map. A way to reflect on how they show up, and a tool to design conversations that move people and systems forward. Figure I.1 introduces the two perspectives that will guide us through this book, an internal view of how we show up in conversations, and an external view of what those conversations are for. Like a pair of lenses, they work best when used together.

Why This Book? Why You?

This book is written for project leaders, change strategists, and senior executives who want to lead with more purpose, clarity, and connection.

The most effective leaders shift between lenses in real time, checking how they are and what the conversation needs.

Lens 1 INTERNAL View

Lens 2 EXTERNAL View

Perspective
Meaning
Awareness
Perception

Purpose
Action
Impact
Intentionality

How am I showing up?

What is this conversation for?

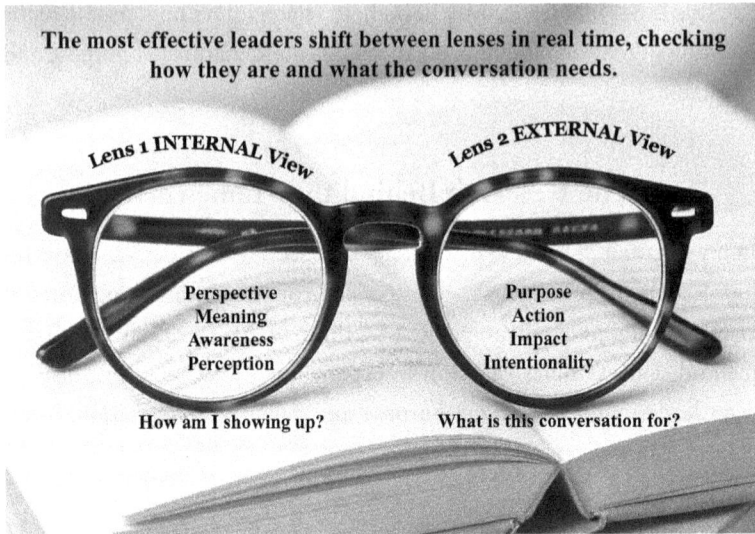

Figure I.1 Dual-Lens leadership: Setting the stage

It's for anyone who has ever left a meeting thinking, "We talked a lot, but did we move forward?" Or faced resistance and wondered, "What conversation aren't we having?"

It's also a call to those leading from within teams, people who may not hold formal titles but are shaping culture through the conversations they choose to start, sustain, or transform. Leadership is not a job title. It's a series of moments. Moments where we invite others into possibility, reframe assumptions, and create space for alignment and change. This book helps you lead those moments well.

What You'll Find Inside

Each chapter in this book is designed to be both practical and reflective. You'll find opening stories featuring three recurring characters from an exciting narrative case study. It is featured across all four books in the Conversations That Inspire Change series:

- Empowering Strategic Change: Conversation-Focused Project Leadership
- Leading Change from Within

- Transformation for People-Centered Leaders
- The Inner Work of Transformation

The WynnTech case highlights a core truth: Transformation is not just about technology but also about people, relationships, and the conversations that make change possible. This story follows the experience of three interconnected leaders—a project manager, a change leader, and an executive—who navigate a high-stakes transformation effort with empathy, reflection, and purpose.

Nia Thompson—Project Lead

Nia Thompson is a detail-oriented and driven project leader, trusted for her ability to keep complex initiatives moving forward under pressure. Known for her commitment to deadlines and deliverables, she excels at coordinating people, processes, and resources. At WynnTech, Nia often finds herself balancing her focus on execution with the need to engage more deeply in the relational and meaning-making aspects of change. Her perspective offers insight into the day-to-day realities and tensions that project leaders face when navigating both timelines and team dynamics.

Marcus Lee—Change Strategist

Marcus Lee brings a big-picture perspective to WynnTech's transformation efforts, drawing on expertise in organizational development and human-centered change. He thrives on uncovering underlying patterns, helping teams make sense of uncertainty, and building trust across diverse groups. Marcus's work highlights the strategic role of conversation in shaping culture, aligning stakeholders, and sustaining momentum during complex change. His approach reflects the nuance and adaptability required of change leaders working at the intersection of people and strategy.

Elena Patel—Executive Leader

As a senior executive, Elena Patel operates at the intersection of vision and accountability, tasked with steering WynnTech toward its long-term strategic goals. She is respected for her decisiveness and high standards yet aware of the pressure this can create for her teams. In moments of change, Elena must navigate the delicate balance between directing outcomes and fostering psychological safety. Her leadership journey reveals how executive presence, trust-building, and vulnerability influence an organization's capacity to transform.

The full WynnTech case study described below provides the complete context and narrative arc of Nia, Marcus, and Elena's work together during a high-stakes transformation.

The WynnTech Case Study

The Context

WynnTech, a midsize technology firm with a respected legacy, embarked on a digital transformation aimed at overhauling outdated systems, improving responsiveness, and fostering a more agile and inclusive culture. Early in the initiative, however, it became clear that this was not merely a technical upgrade but a human journey. Success would depend on aligning hearts and minds as much as platforms and processes.

Three Roles in Reflective Leadership

Nia Thompson—Project Leadership

Nia, the project manager, brought an inclusive lens to delivery. She introduced adaptive governance models, created cross-functional planning teams, and embedded feedback loops that prioritized equity and psychological safety. When middle managers expressed concern about a perceived top-down approach, Nia adjusted timelines and opened up new channels for dialogue. By slowing down to listen, she enabled others to step into ownership and aligned project delivery with people-first values.

Marcus Lee—Change Leadership

Marcus, the change leader, served as the strategic storyteller of the transformation. He facilitated dialogue sessions that helped teams articulate fears, revisit past failures, and cocreate a forward-looking narrative. Drawing on tools from Empowering Strategic Change: Conversation-focused Project Leadership, Marcus reframed the effort from "systems implementation" to "purposeful evolution." His use of metaphor and emotion made space for deeper engagement and helped teams connect with the meaning behind the change.

Elena Patel—Executive Leadership

As WynnTech's COO, Elena initially focused on adoption metrics, efficiencies, and timelines. Through executive coaching and guided reflection, she began to shift her focus inward. Inspired by practices from The Inner Work of Transformation, she embraced vulnerability, hosted monthly learning playbacks, and reframed her role from directive leader to learning partner. Her personal growth journey helped model a new kind of leadership, one grounded in emotional intelligence, humility, and presence.

Bringing It All Together

Together, Nia, Marcus, and Elena created a powerful model of integrated leadership. Their alignment, grounded in shared purpose and reflective practice, helped the transformation take root in meaningful and sustainable ways:

- Strategy was communicated through values-based narrative.
- Systems became more inclusive, flexible, and responsive.
- Psychological safety moved from aspiration to daily practice.
- Inner development was embraced as a driver of organizational change.

Outcomes:

- Twenty-two percent increase in employee engagement
- Faster adoption of digital tools with fewer rework cycles
- Reduced resistance and increased trust in leadership
- Emergence of cross-functional change champions

WynnTech's story now serves as a guiding case across all four books in the series, demonstrating how project, change, and executive leaders can integrate outer strategy with inner clarity, and conversation with action. You will also find in each chapter:

- Research-based insights and frameworks
- Conversation tools, scripts, and reflective prompts
- Case-in-practice examples and narrative tools for team learning

Within each chapter, to support clarity and consistency in reflective practice, each "Leadership Reflection Break" features a leadership quote drawn from conversations with leaders across a wide range of projects and industries. These real-world insights, gathered through consulting engagements and project implementations, reinforce the Dual-Lens Framework by illustrating how leaders experience and apply purposeful conversation in diverse organizational contexts.

Throughout, we return to the central belief that conversation is the engine of transformation. When leaders become more intentional about how they talk, listen, respond, and reflect, they unlock change that is not only implemented but sustained.

Rethinking Leadership: Beyond Role and Rank

While this book focuses on project leaders, change leaders, and strategic or executive leaders, its core message is broader: Leadership is not defined by title but instead by impact. It's about how we show up in moments of uncertainty, how we invite others into meaning-making, and how we move from intention to action in partnership with others. Whether you hold formal authority or lead from within a team, you influence change through the conversations you choose to have, or avoid. Leadership in this book is not confined to the boardroom or the project steering committee. It's present in every interaction where direction is clarified, trust is built, or transformation begins. The tools, stories, and frameworks you'll encounter are meant to be tried, adapted, and made your own. So bring your experience, your questions, and your curiosity, and let's begin the conversation.

KCS

An Invitation to Reflective Leadership

This is also not just a book about talking. It's about becoming the kind of leader whose words carry weight, not because they are polished but because they are authentic, intentional, and aligned with purpose.

As you read, I invite you to bring your lived experience to these pages. Let the tools challenge your habits. Let the stories affirm your instincts. Let the framework stretch your thinking. Most of all, let this book be a companion to the real, reflective work of leadership.

Welcome to the conversation.

KCS

CHAPTER 1

The Evolving Role of the Project Leader

Opening Scene: When Busy Doesn't Mean Forward

The team had been sprinting for weeks, but without pausing to reflect, no one could see whether their actions aligned with the change they wanted to create.

Nia sat alone at her desk long after the office had emptied. The soft glow of her project dashboard bathed the room in blue light. Everything looked good on paper, milestones ticked off, budget tracking steady, risks mitigated. Yet the silence from her team echoed louder than any red flag. The last two meetings had been quiet. Too quiet. No pushback. No enthusiasm. Just … compliance.

She stared at the screen, willing it to tell her something she didn't already know. Her phone buzzed. A text from Marcus: "Still meeting at Café Cornerstone? Elena's already there."

Nia grabbed her coat and headed out into the cool evening air, hoping the change of scenery might clear her thoughts. At the café, she spotted Marcus waving from a corner booth. Elena sat beside him, half-listening to a podcast through one earbud and scribbling notes in the margin of a leadership book.

As Nia slid into the seat across from them, she didn't wait for pleasantries.

"I feel like I'm managing a ghost project," she said quietly. "Everything's moving … but the energy's gone. It's like we're going through the motions."

Marcus nodded slowly. "What kind of conversations are you having with the team?"

Nia hesitated. "Mostly status updates. Deadlines. Risk mitigation. The usual."

Elena closed her notebook. "And what kind of leadership do you think that signals, especially when you sense something's off?"

The question hit hard. Nia looked down at her coffee.

"I've been managing the plan, not the people."

A long silence followed—not uncomfortable but charged. Marcus leaned in.

"What if the problem isn't the project? What if it's the conversations we're not having?"

That question shifted something in Nia, not in the schedule, but in herself. For the first time in weeks, she wasn't thinking about delivery. She was thinking about connection. That evening didn't end with a revised Gantt chart or new action items. But it marked the start of a deeper inquiry, one that would change how Nia led, how her team engaged, and how the transformation unfolded.

Let's get into the chapter and the evolving role of the project leader.

Conversation as a Core Leadership Practice

This chapter begins by making the case for a new kind of project leader, one who balances technical skill with reflection, adaptability, and a human-centered mindset. In today's evolving landscape, project leadership isn't just about delivering results. It's about how we grow, learn, and lead through complexity, collaboration, and change. At the heart of this shift is a simple but powerful idea: effective leadership is grounded not only in execution but in the quality of our conversations.

"Leadership conversations guide the change."

Project and change leaders are frequently evaluated by what they deliver, meeting deadlines, achieving milestones, and keeping initiatives on track. But when the goal is to foster true commitment, shift perspectives, and keep people engaged through uncertainty, it's not the plan that leads but instead the story behind it.

So let's begin this chapter with a fundamental idea: Strategic leadership takes shape through the conversations we have every day. The words we choose, the stories we tell, and the shared meaning we build in dialogue are what shape how others experience change, develop trust, and take ownership of progress.

Conversations are how leaders:

- Turn strategy into meaningful action.
- Bring focus and clarity to competing demands.
- Reveal challenges and uncover insight.
- Maintain energy and commitment through change.

The Research Behind the Practice

As introduced in the opening of this book, my doctoral research explored how senior leaders make sense of their leadership conversations during times of organizational change. Returning to that foundation here in Chapter 1, we go deeper into what I learned through a qualitative methodology known as phenomenography. Rather than focusing solely on what leaders said, this research surfaced how they experienced the meaning and purpose of conversation within their roles.

Through interviews across diverse business contexts, five distinct ways of understanding leadership dialogue emerged, each representing a different perspective on how leaders engage with change through conversation. These insights form the foundation of what we now refer to as Lens 1: Experience in the Dual-Lens Framework:

1. Strategically Intentional—**D**elivering direction, ensuring compliance
2. Catalyst for Change—**S**parking insight and new pathways
3. Mindful Awareness—**C**ocreating meaning and reflection in real time
4. Building Shared Commitment—**B**uilding trust, authenticity, and accountability
5. Guiding the Change—**L**eading fundamental shifts in direction or identity

Each of these distinct ways of understanding conversations reflects increasing levels of leadership awareness and potential for impact.

The purpose of this research was to build a deeper and broader under-standing of how senior leaders experience and interpret their leadership conversations during organizational change initiatives. This work was designed to advance understanding of how leadership conversations con-tributed to organizational change theory. It emphasized that each leader's experience reflected an internal relationship between the individual and the phenomenon of leadership conversation itself.

Study Reveals Business Value

Leaders within an organization have various intentions and reasons to com-municate: to provide information, to implement a change, to influence and motivate employees to perform better, to make decisions, to reward and recognize, to resolve conflict, and to coach and counsel. Knowing their con-versations are instrumental in influencing the relationships and behaviors of their employees and team members provides insight into:

- The role of conversation as a critical mechanism for planning communication implementations during change
- The role conversation plays in affecting the outcome of an organi-zational change initiative, which is essential for providing greater flexibility for leaders to respond faster to changes in their business
- The extent to which change conversations can help to decrease anxiety, increase motivation, and support the adoption of the be-haviors or activities needed to achieve the desired outcome

Introducing the Dual-Lens Framework

To support leaders in navigating these conversations, this book introduces a Dual-Lens Conversation Framework that brings together two powerful models:

- Categories of Experience (the lived experience of leaders in conversation)
- Functional Conversation Types (the strategic purpose behind each dialogue)

This framework offers leaders both reflection and direction: a way to see how their conversations are experienced, and a guide to engage more purposefully and clearly in future dialogue.

Lens 1 Focus

Lens 1 focuses on five different categories that represent how senior leaders make meaning of leadership conversations, what it means to the leader, what leaders are thinking about, what they are trying to do, and what they want to achieve.

This framework has provided advanced understanding in that change is created by:

- Understanding audience perspectives and changing the conversation to suit the outcomes
- A step-by-step process of conversations, creating shared understandings leading to more comprehensive levels of meaning
- Conversations that influence strategic processes leading to transformational outcomes

There was a clearer understanding of how leader's conversations influenced business change and a greater appreciation for how closely their conversational behaviors influenced the leadership of change in the business.

Figure 1.1 shows how leaders internally experience their conversations, ranging from acting as Strategically Intentional, Catalyst for Change, Mindful Awareness, and Building Shared Commitment to Guiding the Change, reflecting their awareness, intentions, and relational stance.

The research findings (summarized in Table 1.1) provided new knowledge for practitioners and leaders, like yourselves, engaging in developing, designing, and implementing organizational change.

Lens 2 Focus

Lens 2 focuses on what leaders aim to achieve through conversation. It breaks down leadership dialogue into five core functions: delivering

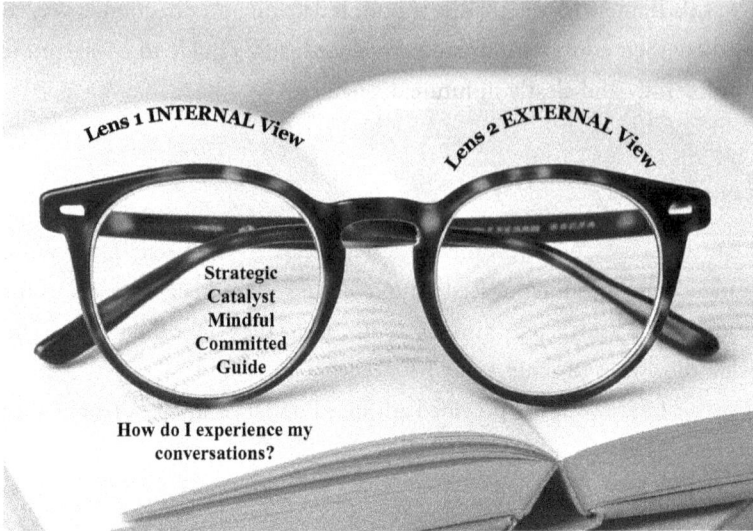

Figure 1.1 Lens 1—A leader's internal view

Table 1.1 Lens 1: Categories of experience leadership conversations

Category name	Description
Category 1 Strategically Intentional	Leadership conversations are experienced as strategically intentional to influence others.
Category 2 Catalyst for Change	Leadership conversations give leaders new insights and are a means of creating new pathways of possibilities.
Category 3 Mindful Awareness	Leadership conversations are mindful, a process of continually orienting, adjusting and creating opportunities for deeper, more meaningful possibilities.
Category 4 Building Shared Commitment	Leadership conversations develop genuine relationships based on authenticity, foster a sense of personal accountability, and build shared commitment.
Category 5 Guiding the Change	Leadership conversations help lead an organization to do something significantly or fundamentally different from what they have done before.

Derived from phenomenographic research, these categories represent how leaders experience their conversations.

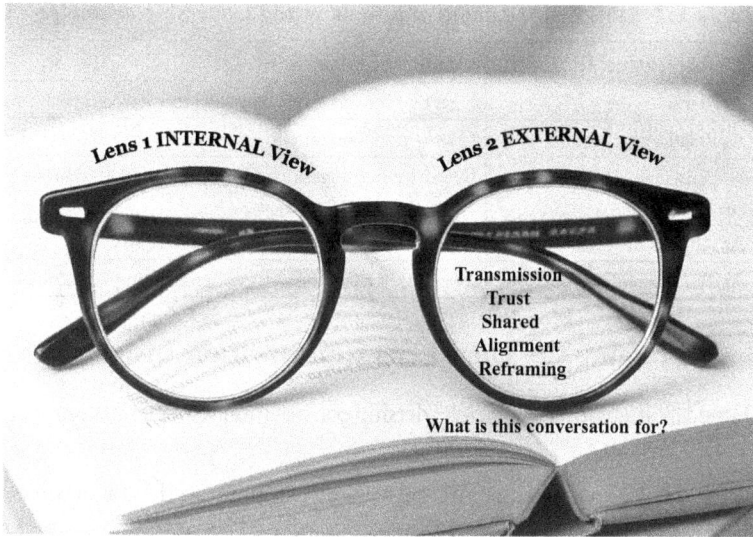

Figure 1.2 Lens 2—A leader's external view

direction (Transmission), building trust (Relationship), helping others make sense of change (Sensemaking), connecting people to purpose (Alignment), and reshaping how people see themselves and their roles (Transformation).

Figure 1.2 focuses on the strategic purpose of conversations, whether the goal is Transmission, Building Trust, Creating Shared Understanding, Driving Alignment, or Reframing perspectives to enable transformation.

These are not just communication styles but also intentional actions that support strategic outcomes. Research by Rizvi and Popli (2021) shows that leadership communication drives behavior and reinforces transformation, while Souza and Wood (2022) argue that effective leadership adapts across individual and collective levels. Together, these insights affirm Lens 2 as a practical framework (outlined in Table 1.2) for guiding purposeful conversations that move people and change forward.

Together, these studies validate Lens 2 as a practical model for external, purposive dialogue, extending the strategic utility of leadership conversation in complex, people-centered change initiatives.

Table 1.2 Lens 2: Conversation functions and leadership examples

Conversation function	Leadership example
As Transmission	Directive conversations that align task execution
As Relationship	Check-ins or one-on-one conversations that build trust
As Sensemaking	Reflective meetings or coaching conversations that create shared understanding
As Alignment	Strategic storytelling or alignment sessions
As Transformation	Visioning or reframing conversations that inspire possibility

Framing the Dual-Lens Conversation Insights

Table 1.3 illustrates how each leadership conversation serves a dual purpose:

- Lens 1 captures the internal stance or mindset of the leader, how they experience their role, their intent, and what meaning they assign to the conversation.
- Lens 2 reveals the strategic function of the conversation, how it is used as a purposeful intervention to influence, align, or shift behavior in the context of change.

The Leadership Examples in the table demonstrate how these two lenses come together in real practice. These are not merely transactional communications but moments of leadership insight, where the leader's self-awareness informs how they intentionally shape conversations to meet evolving project needs. These are the "gray zone" conversations where reflective action leads to transformative outcomes.

Gray zones are the ambiguous, emotionally charged, and often unstructured moments that arise during change, when priorities conflict, clarity dissolves, and established norms no longer apply. These are the spaces where technical plans fall short and human dynamics take center stage.

In the **Dual-Lens Framework**, gray zones are where both lenses become essential:

- **Lens 1 (Experience)** helps leaders tune into their internal responses and the emotional undercurrents within the team, fear, resistance, confusion, or hope.

Table 1.3 Dual-Lens combined framework

Phenomenographic category (Lens 1)	Conversation function (Lens 2)	Leadership example (Dual-Lens insight)
Strategically Intentional	As Transmission	Directive conversations that align task execution
Catalyst for Change	As Transformation	Visioning or reframing conversations that inspire possibility
Mindful Awareness	As Sensemaking	Reflective meetings or coaching conversations that create shared understanding
Building Shared Commitment	As Relationship	Check-ins or one-on-one conversations that build trust
Guiding the Change	As Alignment/ Transformation	Strategic storytelling or alignment sessions

- **Lens 2 (Function)** guides leaders to choose the right kind of conversation, whether to clarify, align, relate, or transform, based on what the moment calls for.

Leading in gray zones requires more than delivering information; it demands awareness, adaptability, and intentional dialogue that bridges uncertainty with meaning. In complex or ambiguous project environments, effective leaders navigate fluently between the two lenses, recognizing that their internal experience of the moment profoundly influences the conversations they initiate and the actions they take.

Dual-Lens Framework: Leadership Experience and Function

The Dual-Lens Framework illustrates how each leadership conversation serves a dual purpose: Lens 1 reflects the internal stance or mindset of the leader, how they experience their role and understand the conversation's meaning. Lens 2 represents the strategic function of the conversation, how it is used as a purposeful intervention to support change. The leadership examples provided in Table 1.3 demonstrate how reflective insight (Lens 1) and strategic intent (Lens 2) are combined in real project contexts.

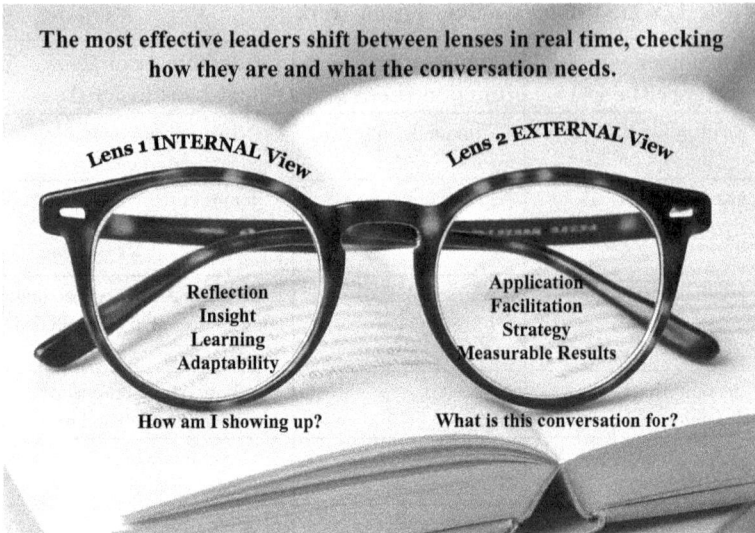

Figure 1.3 Understanding the Dual-Lens perspective

The Dual-Lens Framework is most powerful when both lenses are viewed in tandem. Lens 1 offers insight into the internal world of the leader, the beliefs, emotions, and experiences that shape how they show up. But awareness alone is not enough. To lead effectively through change, that inner clarity must be translated into intentional external action. This is where Lens 2 comes into play, providing a practical structure for understanding how leadership conversations function as strategic tools in dynamic, people-centered environments.

Figure 1.3 integrates the internal and external views, showing how leaders balance personal experience with intentional, outcome-driven conversation design.

Reframing Leadership Conversation in Complex Environments

This Dual-Lens Framework advances phenomenographic research by linking subjective insight with observable impact. It bridges leadership theory with business and project practice, providing a flexible, scalable framework for reflection, facilitation, and development. In today's complex environments, there is growing recognition that leadership con- versation must evolve, from a communication tactic to a core strategic intervention.

This evolution in leadership dialogue is precisely what the Dual-Lens Framework is designed to support, connecting a leader's internal aware- ness with their external impact. As leadership conversations shift from tactical exchanges to strategic interventions, the framework offers a way to navigate that complexity with intentionality and insight.

This shift is reinforced by research: Psychological safety (Edmond- son 2019) highlights how the tone and emotional quality of conversation shape innovation and risk-taking. Systems thinking (Senge 2006) fur- ther emphasizes the power of dialogue to surface hidden interdependen- cies and foster collective sensemaking, core functions embedded in the Dual-Lens Framework.

The framework is a continuation of my academic inquiry and a re- sponse to the demands of modern leadership. It presents a practical, research-informed approach, grounded in both best practice research and lived experience, for guiding change through intentional dialogue. This equips leaders, teams, and educators with a shared language to reflect, adapt, and cocreate more human-centered, aligned, and transformative outcomes.

Serving as both a mirror and a map, the framework supports reflective practice by helping leaders assess the underlying purpose and impact of their conversations. It also introduces a practical vocabulary for coaching, designing interventions, and navigating complexity with greater inten- tion and clarity.

By adopting this Dual-Lens Framework, project, change, and execu- tive leaders can cultivate a more adaptive and responsive conversational style, one that shifts fluidly across communication types based on team needs, project phases, and the emotional dynamics of the organization.

From Execution to Meaning-Making: The Conversation That Changed Everything

A senior project leader I once coached, let's call her Chapelle, was re- sponsible for implementing a new digital intake system in a large health network. The tech was solid. The project plan was tight. But halfway through rollout, the team was burned out, clinicians were skeptical, and change fatigue was real.

In a debrief session, Chapelle said, "I've done everything right on paper, but it's not landing. It's like I'm managing a project no one wants."

So, we paused the push. Chapelle hosted a series of small group conversations, not to convince, but to listen. She asked: "What are we not hearing?" and "What's this change asking of us emotionally?"

In one session, a nurse said, "This isn't about software. It's about losing the way we've always done care." Another added, "It feels like efficiency over empathy."

That changed everything. Chapelle shifted from managing resistance to hosting dialogue. She integrated these stories into project updates, gave voice to frontline insights, and repositioned the system not just as efficient but as compassionate. The rollout didn't speed up, but it stuck. What moved the needle was not a better system spec. It was a better conversation.

Evolving Leadership Conversations in the Age of Digital Transformation

Traditional project management, with its structured, linear methodologies like Waterfall, Critical Path Method, and PRINCE2, have long served as the backbone of delivery for predictable, well-scoped initiatives. Traditional project management emphasized structure, consistency, and delivery. It was born in engineering and tech, where control and certainty were prized. But in today's environment, marked by rapid technological change, evolving user expectations, and continuous disruption, these models often fall short. Digital transformation, in particular, demands more than process adherence; it requires agility, cocreation, and the courage to lead through uncertainty.

For **project leaders**, this means more than adopting Agile frameworks or new tools. It means learning to lead conversations that surface emergent needs, support iterative planning, and continuously engage stakeholders. It's no longer sufficient to define scope and lock in deliverables upfront. Project leaders must be fluent in negotiating shifting priorities, testing assumptions in real time, and translating abstract visions into actionable steps, often without a clear roadmap.

For **change leaders**, the work lies in cultivating cultural readiness. They must use conversation to uncover hidden resistance, foster emotional buy-in, and connect the "why" of transformation to the everyday realities of teams. Change leaders are responsible not just for communication plans but for creating space where people can question, interpret, and internalize new ways of working. Their dialogues must be open, responsive, and grounded in empathy.

And for **business or executive leaders**, transformation cannot simply be handed down as a set of strategic imperatives. Leadership at this level must involve aligning the organization around a shared purpose and a flexible vision, then communicating that vision not just through formal channels but through everyday moments that reinforce direction and invite adaptation. Strategic conversations at the top set the tone for everything that follows: clarity, transparency, and the willingness to acknowledge what's unknown all ripple through the system.

If we attempt to apply legacy methods to emerging technologies and uncertain conditions, we risk stalled delivery, organizational fatigue, and solutions that are obsolete before they're fully deployed. The success rate of digital transformation projects remains alarmingly low, not due to technical failure but due to misalignment, inflexibility, and breakdowns in communication.

To shift this pattern, leaders at every level must rethink the role of conversation. Rather than using dialogue to simply transmit decisions, they must use it to sense, adapt, and cocreate. This means being comfortable with shifting scope, redefining deliverables, and engaging in iterative learning cycles. It also means recognizing that tools and technology alone will not drive success, culture, mindset, and leadership presence will.

In this new era, project leadership is not just about managing tasks but also about stewarding transformation through conversation. Digital tools can help streamline workflows and enhance visibility, but it's the reflective, inclusive, and future-focused conversations that enable real progress.

Today's projects live in different contexts. In health care, education, public policy, and social innovation, leaders must navigate:

- Competing priorities and ambiguous goals
- Diverse teams with lived experience
- Constant stakeholder input and public scrutiny

Success isn't just about scope, time, and budget. It's about trust, alignment, and adaptability.

The modern project leader is no longer just an executor. They are a facilitator of meaning, a translator of vision, and a host of emotionally complex conversations. They are, in many ways, a narrative architect.

Why Reflection Matters Now

We are leading in a time of profound complexity and continuous disruption. Volatility and rapid technological shifts are redefining industries and resetting expectations overnight. Hybrid and decentralized teams are reshaping how we collaborate, connect, and make decisions across distance and difference. There are rising calls for justice, inclusion, and well-being that are pushing leaders to reexamine not just how they lead but why.

In this environment, project leaders can no longer rely on static plans or one-size-fits-all solutions. Instead, they must lead with agility, humility, and a commitment to learning in real time. Reflection is no longer a luxury reserved for post-project reviews; it is a daily discipline. It means pausing, even briefly, to ask:

- What's working?
- What's shifting?
- Who's not at the table?
- What's the story beneath the status report?

Reflective leadership builds resilience by helping teams metabolize uncertainty rather than avoid it. It normalizes adaptation, making change feel navigable instead of chaotic. And perhaps most importantly, it creates space for honesty, humanity, and healing, especially in moments of tension, fatigue, or disconnection.

By practicing reflection in motion, project leaders signal that uncertainty is not a threat to be managed, but a condition to be explored. They create cultures where learning is visible, feedback is valued, and people feel safe to question, imagine, and grow.

Defining the Reflective Project Leader

The reflective project leader isn't a new job title, it's a new way of showing up. They:

- Balance execution with introspection.
- Prioritize relationships alongside results.
- Stay grounded in uncertainty.
- Model curiosity and learning.
- They don't see conversation as a formality. They see it as a core leadership act.

When reflective leaders speak, they:

- Pause instead of push.
- Ask instead of assume.
- Name tensions instead of avoiding them.
- They invite shared authorship of both the process and the outcome.

Leadership Conversation Reflection Workbook

A workbook has been designed to support reflective leadership practice across three key roles: executive leaders, change leaders, and project leaders. Each section offers a structured worksheet to guide you through recent or upcoming leadership conversations, helping you reflect on both the internal experience of the dialogue and its strategic purpose. These tools can be used independently or with a coach, and are especially valuable during moments of complexity, transition, or transformation. Complete each section based on your role or explore all three to deepen your understanding of how leadership conversations shape outcomes, relationships, and organizational change. Leaders can locate this workbook in Appendix A: Leadership Conversation Workbook (Tool 1); however, let's look at an illustration.

Example in Practice: A Case from the Field

The following case study serves as a unifying thread throughout this book and future volumes in this series, offering a consistent reference point to explore how leaders navigate real-world transformation. It highlights the interplay between strategic leadership and operational execution, while integrating key concepts introduced in each chapter. By returning to a shared case across multiple chapters, readers can build a deeper, more connected understanding of leadership conversations and practice over time. A complete version of the case study is also included in the Ancillaries section.

Case Study: The WynnTech Transformation—Reflective Leadership in Action

As digital transformation initiatives accelerate across industries, leaders often find themselves pulled between competing priorities: technical delivery, stakeholder alignment, and cultural change. The WynnTech case offers a vivid illustration of how project, change, and executive leadership, when practiced reflectively, can align to move transformation from intention to impact.

A Narrative Example of a Real Project and Change Initiative

WynnTech, a midsize technology firm, launched a major digital transformation aimed at modernizing systems and building a more agile, inclusive culture. While the technical goals were clear, the organization soon discovered that the real challenge lay in navigating cultural resistance, leadership misalignment, and emotional fatigue.

At the center were three leaders, Nia (Project Lead), Marcus (Change Strategist), and Elena (Executive Leader), each playing a distinct but interdependent role in the transformation.

Nia embedded inclusive project governance by creating cross-functional planning teams and feedback loops that supported equity and psychological safety. When resistance emerged, she adjusted timelines and created space for open dialogue.

Marcus reframed the initiative through reflective conversations and strategic storytelling. His work helped people name their fears, reframe the narrative, and build emotional engagement with the change.

Elena transitioned from a metrics-focused executive to a learning-oriented leader. Through business coaching and reflective practice, she modeled vulnerability and hosted leadership dialogues that created cultural permission for authenticity.

How Reflective Project Leadership Made a Difference

Nia's shift from task management to reflective facilitation enabled the project to proceed with greater buy-in and less burnout. Rather than pushing through resistance, she paused to understand it. By focusing on conversation as a leadership act, Nia helped surface concerns that would have otherwise derailed the transformation.

Marcus used sensemaking and relationship-centered conversation to bridge emotional gaps in the organization. His leadership demonstrated how change doesn't land because it's mandated, it lands because it's interpreted, coauthored, and internalized.

Elena's example showed how executive leadership, when grounded in inner work and emotional presence, sets the tone for psychological safety and adaptive capacity across the organization.

What This Case Reveals About Reflective Leadership

This case will illustrate the power of reflective leadership across all levels of transformation:

- Conversation as a strategy: Change was enabled not by directive communication, but by generative, emotionally intelligent dialogue.
- Inner work fuels outer results: The leaders' willingness to self-reflect led to more inclusive processes, adaptive planning, and a healthier organizational culture.
- Alignment across roles matters: When project, change, and executive leaders are united in purpose and reflective practice, transformation becomes more sustainable and humane.

WynnTech's journey reminds us that successful transformation is never just technical. It is cultural, relational, and deeply personal. Reflective project leadership is not a luxury; rather, it's a necessity in the face of complexity.

Reflective Prompts

Think of a project you led or supported. What kind of leadership did the project require, and what kind of leadership did it reveal in you?

Think back to a recent leadership conversation:

- What were you trying to achieve?
- How did it land with others?
- What kind of conversation was it: transmission, relationship, sensemaking, alignment, transformation?

Reflective Case in Practice: Navigating the Gray Zone

In a climate where volatility, pressure, and pace dominate, leadership often defaults to control. But meaningful progress in transformation requires something different: the courage to pause, reflect, and reframe.

In this case, the cross-departmental team was tasked with implementing a new intake process to streamline services and advance equity. The project was already behind schedule.

Nia, the project lead, was focused on deliverables and trying to keep everything moving forward.

Marcus, the change lead, had been brought in to improve engagement but found himself pushing messages more than fostering dialogue.

Elena, the senior leader, was under pressure from above and growing impatient with the pace of change.

Tensions mounted. A team meeting ended with visible frustration. Staff felt unheard. Managers disengaged. The mood reflected more than a missed milestone; it revealed a misalignment in approach and understanding.

The three leaders regrouped. What began as a tactical debrief slowly became a reflective conversation. Nia admitted that she was relying on process as a shield, avoiding the difficult interpersonal work. Marcus recognized that he had underestimated how deeply power dynamics were shaping staff silence. Elena acknowledged that her fear of being perceived as ineffective was leading her to overcontrol.

They stepped back. Slowed down. Asked different questions. They reframed expectations, not just about timelines but about how success would be measured. They held intentional space for dialogue and emotion, allowing new insights to emerge.

What resulted wasn't just a revised project plan. It was a shared commitment to lead differently, through trust, self-awareness, and connection. The team moved forward not just with clearer roles but with a stronger relational foundation.

This is the work of reflective leadership in action: shifting from urgency to understanding, from task focus to meaning-making. Especially in the gray zones of change, reflection is what turns tension into insight and fragmentation into forward motion.

Applying the Reflective Practice Worksheet: Three Perspectives from the Gray Zone

To illustrate how the Leadership Conversation Reflection Worksheet can be used in practice, leaders can find the worksheet in Appendix A, let's visit the Gray Zone case through the lens of each leader. This tool supports reflection in four parts: context, dual-lens analysis, personal insights, and next steps. Here's how it might have looked:

Nia, Our Project Lead

Part 1: Conversation Overview
Purpose: Debrief project delays and misalignment.
Stakeholders: Cross-departmental team, Marcus (change strategist), Elena (senior leader).
Context: High urgency, delayed delivery, disengaged staff.

Part 2: Dual-Lens Reflection
Internal Experience: Focused on process, avoided deeper conversations.

Conversation Function: Primarily transmission, driving updates and timelines.

Realization: Avoiding emotional discomfort was limiting team trust and ownership.

Part 3: Insight
Leadership required: Courage to lean into discomfort.
Missed opportunity: Sensing emotional undercurrents.

Part 4: Next Step
Strengthen the habit of pausing to ask "What are we not saying?"
Revisit conversations with key staff to rebuild relational trust.

Marcus, Our Change Strategist

Part 1: Overview
Purpose: Increase staff engagement.
Context: High resistance, unclear sponsorship.

Part 2: Dual-Lens
Internal: Frustrated, underestimating how hierarchy silences input.
Function: Intended transformation, but defaulted to transmission.

Part 3: Insight
Leadership required: Creating safe space for hard truths.
Shift: From persuading to co-sensing.

Part 4: Action
Design future conversations around sensemaking prompts, not directives.
Encourage team-led story-sharing about the impact of change.

Elena, Our Executive Leader

Part 1: Overview
Purpose: Understand delays, maintain strategic momentum.
Context: High-level pressure, urgency to show outcomes.

Part 2: Dual-Lens
Internal: Fear of failure, masking with control.
Function: Meant to align, but came off as rigid transmission.

Part 3: Insight
Leadership required: Modeling vulnerability to unlock team learning.
Realization: Pressure was leading to rigidity, not results.

Part 4: Action
Name the tension in leadership meetings.
Normalize reflection moments in project updates (e.g., "What are we learning?").

Why This Matters

These reflections show how leaders in different roles and at different levels can engage with the same situation from diverse vantage points, and still arrive at aligned, growth-oriented insights. The worksheet doesn't just help surface lessons; it creates accountability for more conscious, adaptive leadership conversations going forward. By using this tool consistently, leaders build muscle for real-time learning, deeper alignment, and resilience through complexity.

Introducing the Three Anchors: Practice, Pedagogy, and Purpose

To support this shift in leadership, this book introduces a foundational trio that forms the backbone of reflective project leadership: **Practice, Pedagogy, and Purpose**. These anchors provide a balanced framework that connects what leaders do, how they learn, and why it matters.

Practice refers to the applied tools, routines, and habits that leaders use to guide teams and deliver results. This includes methods such as stand-up meetings, retrospectives, stakeholder mapping, and decision-making frameworks. But it also includes the micro-practices, listening deeply, pausing before responding, and modeling vulnerability, that shape the tone and culture of a team.

Pedagogy speaks to how leaders design for learning, reflection, and inclusion within the project environment. It recognizes that every project is also a learning experience, and that leaders must be intentional about how they facilitate understanding, support diverse ways of knowing, and cultivate psychological safety. Pedagogy is about being a facilitator of growth, not just a manager of tasks.

Purpose is the anchor that connects work to meaning. It asks: Why does this project matter? How does it align with our values and the broader systems we're part of? Purpose helps leaders frame challenges in context, sustain motivation through complexity, and make decisions that reflect more than efficiency, it reflects ethics and impact.

Together, these anchors help reflective project leaders:

- Act with clarity: grounded in tools and routines that serve their goals.
- Create space for growth: by designing environments that support learning and inclusion.
- Lead with integrity: by staying rooted in values and connected to a deeper mission.

As the following chapters unfold, each anchor will reappear in different forms, embedded in tools, stories, and reflective practices, providing a scaffold for developing your own leadership approach that is both strategic and human-centered.

Reflective Prompts

Think of a time when you knew what needed to be done in a project or change effort, but the challenge was in how to lead others through it. What did that experience teach you about the difference between knowledge and leadership presence?

Learning Outcomes

The following outcomes summarize the knowledge and skills you've developed in this chapter:

- Explain the Dual-Lens Framework and its role in connecting internal leadership experience (Lens 1) with external strategic purpose (Lens 2).
- Identify the five categories of leadership conversation from Lens 1 and describe how they shape meaning-making during change.
- Apply the Leadership Conversation Reflection Workbook (Tool 1) to analyze a recent or upcoming conversation in your own context.
- Recognize the value of intentional dialogue as a core leadership practice, not just a communication skill.

A Glimpse Ahead

In the chapters to come, we'll dive deeper into the Dual-Lens Framework, exploring how leaders can move between types of conversation with greater intention and impact. We'll explore topics such as:

- How to lead through conversations using the Dual-Lens Framework, integrating both internal experience and strategic function
- How to use storytelling as a strategic tool
- How to become a narrative leader who builds purpose, not just compliance
- How to design reflective moments in project and change work

---

"Leadership Reflection Break"

"There is real possibility in creating breakthroughs/being innovative with change, using structure and bringing in the right people. We were the first to create conversations because we brought all the people into the same room, all the stakeholders into one room to discuss the challenges and impacts to the company using this structured approach to conversation, we did this through conversations."

CHAPTER 2

The Dual-Lens Framework—Linking Experience with Function

Opening Scene: The Strategy That Fell Flat

Everyone had nodded during the presentation, but without connecting strategy to meaning, the vision failed to take root.

Marcus stood at the front of the conference room, the final slide of his change strategy on display behind him. The managers in the room offered polite nods and vague expressions, but the air felt heavy. The energy, like the engagement, was flat.

He had spent weeks crafting this presentation: achieving clear direction and thoughtful sequencing, and grounding every piece in logic. But when the floor opened for discussion, the response was tepid: a few clarifying questions. No challenge, and no curiosity, either. It was the kind of silence that didn't reassure; it was unsettled.

Later that afternoon, Marcus joined Nia and Elena in the small conference room near the leadership suite. He dropped into a chair with a sigh.

"I gave them clarity," he said, frustration simmering beneath the words. "But it's like they weren't even in the room."

Elena tilted her head. "Maybe clarity wasn't what they needed."

Nia added gently, "We keep assuming that alignment means agreement. But alignment has a heartbeat, it needs emotional buy-in, not just direction."

Marcus looked at them, the weight of realization sinking in. He had delivered a strategy, not a conversation. The plan had made sense, but it hadn't connected.

As they unpacked the meeting together, something shifted. They began examining not just what they were saying but how and why. Marcus's comfort with providing direction, Elena's instinct for certainty, Nia's aversion to conflict, all of it shaped the way they led. The question wasn't whether they were communicating. It was whether they were creating meaning.

That conversation marked their first real encounter with the dual-lens idea: that leadership conversations must be understood from the inside out, linking inner awareness with external purpose.

The Dual-Lens Framework: Linking Experience with Function

This chapter introduces a deep dive into the Dual-Lens Framework that integrates how leaders experience conversation (Lens 1: Categories of Experience) and what those conversations are designed to accomplish (Lens 2: Conversational Function). It outlines five categories on each lens and demonstrates how they align to guide leadership action.

"Every conversation we have is a small act of leadership."

When we think about leadership in the context of projects or organizational change, we often think in terms of actions, planning, decision making, risk management. But the most powerful leadership work often happens in conversation. A well-timed question, a thoughtful story, or a moment of deep listening can move a team further than any directive or spreadsheet. This chapter introduces the research-based framework that helps leaders recognize, use, and expand their repertoire of leadership conversations.

Alignment with the Dual-Lens Framework

This chapter offers a clear alignment between the phenomenographic categories of experience and the functional types of conversation, helping readers deepen their understanding of how leadership dialogue works in practice. It invites reflection on how each type is used, and when different combinations may be most effective in leading change.

The Research Behind the Framework

During my doctoral research, I spent time exploring how senior leaders make sense of their conversations during times of change. If you recall, I used a method called phenomenography, an approach that uncovers the different ways people experience the same thing. Through interviews with leaders across various business units, I started to see some clear patterns in how they understood and approached their leadership dialogues. What stood out were five distinct ways of experiencing conversation, each one reflecting a deeper level of intention, complexity, and possibility. These aren't rigid styles or personality types. Instead, they represent different perspectives on what leadership conversations are really for, how they work, and the role they play in leading change.

Lens 1: Categories of Experience

Grounded in qualitative inquiry into leadership experience, these categories form the foundation of Lens 1 in the Dual-Lens Framework. They reflect the internal lens leaders use to interpret conversations, how they make meaning of their roles, relationships, and the situational dynamics unfolding in real time.

Category 1: Strategically Intentional

> *Leadership conversations are experienced as strategically intentional to influence others.*

The core purpose of this category is to highlight how leaders intentionally use dialogue to direct focus and influence specific results. Leaders described their understanding of conversations as purposeful efforts, where talk is about determining how people think about and respond to organizational changes, creating shared experiences through face-to-face conversations, building trust and strengthening relationships. On a continuous basis with individuals and direct report teams, leaders influence the direction of successful organizational change by recognizing individual differences and using diverse types of conversations.

Category 2—Catalyst for Change

Leadership conversations give leaders new insights and are a means of creating new pathways of possibilities.

Leaders understand that the effective conversations they have can lead to higher levels of organizational alignment, improvement toward the relationships within and outside the company and also to deliberately shape the organization's direction. Leadership conversations are instrumental in changing the core culture, direction and motivation needed to succeed in a changing environment. From this perspective, their conversations serve as the catalyst for change. In this category leaders described the "huge amount of commitment" and "dedicated time" required by them to bring their teams together in order to move ahead with change.

Category 3—Mindful Awareness

Leadership conversations are mindful, a process of continually orienting, adjusting, and creating opportunities for deeper, more meaningful possibilities.

The central theme for this category was the ability of leaders to openly discuss their awareness of what they were saying while they said it, and that they were very much aware of the impact of their words. While conversations were purposeful and framed, conversations go where they need to go based on the variety of perspectives and interests in the conversation. This process provides an opportunity to see things from more than one perspective and provides an opportunity for learning for everyone involved in the conversation.

Being mindful is a way of thinking and engaging and paying attention to what matters. Leaders inspire people to be agents of change by seeing things from more than one perspective, and taking in what is new about them, coming to see them in a new light, breaking down barriers.

Category 4—Building Shared Commitment

Leadership conversations develop genuine relationships based on authenticity, foster a sense of personal accountability, and build shared commitment.

In this category leaders experienced intrinsic benefits from their leadership conversations, in terms of enhanced personal meaning. Within this way of experiencing, leaders approached their conversations with a sense of passion, led discussions to focus on key messages, and managed to build understandings around the common vision for the organization.

This category had meaning for senior leaders that they articulated as intimate conversations, the challenge in building understanding and commitment to current goals, and future possibilities. This meant taking the message and not just communicating it across the entire organization but building a genuine relationship with their team and engaging accountability through this dialogue.

Category 5—Guiding the Change

Leadership conversations guide an organization in achieving something significantly or fundamentally different from what they have done before.

Leaders now understand that well developed plans, even plans that contain brilliant strategies, are not enough to ensure success. Change leadership implies that leaders have a responsibility to guide an organization through a course of change by providing direction and support throughout this process. Today's work environment is diverse, complex, and characterized by constant change. When teams lack clear priorities or alignment, or have conflicting agendas, it is difficult to get the necessary understanding to carry strategic initiatives to success.

To reach its full potential, an organization must become aligned so that all processes are moving in the same direction in a concerted approach. It requires a keen understanding of alignment principles, systemic thinking (the ability to perceive, integrate, and align complex systems), and the ability to read and influence individual and group needs, motivations, and commitment. But when leaders share the values and vision with their teams, and when everyone collectively understands the key drivers and the strategies that are being employed to address them, then everyone can be collectively committed to the major strategic efforts of the organization.

Introducing Lens 2: Conversations as Strategic Interventions

In Chapter 1, we introduced the concept of reflective, people-centered leadership and laid the groundwork for viewing leadership conversations as more than interpersonal exchanges. These conversations offer insight into how leaders think, respond, and engage, revealing both personal awareness and relational intention.

Chapter 2 builds on that foundation by expanding the focus from internal reflection to external strategic purpose. It invites us to consider not only how leaders experience conversations but why they engage in them, and what they are trying to achieve in the context of change.

Through qualitative inquiry with leaders across multiple business units, five distinct ways of experiencing leadership dialogue emerged. These weren't fixed communication habits or inherent dispositions. Rather, they reflected evolving perspectives on the role of conversation in shaping meaning, building relationships, and influencing outcomes. This became the foundation for Lens 1.

Over time, I've seen these findings echoed in practice, through coaching engagements, team strategy sessions, and large-scale transformation initiatives. Across sectors and roles, the same five perspectives continue to show up, reinforcing the utility of Lens 1 as a framework for understanding the internal stance leaders bring into dialogue. But inner awareness alone isn't enough.

To lead change effectively, leaders must also be intentional about how their conversations function externally. That's where Lens 2 comes in. It builds upon the insights of Lens 1 and focuses on the strategic purposes of conversation: how leaders use dialogue to direct, connect, clarify, align, and transform.

Lens 2 has been shaped by continued research and best practices across industries. It offers a practical model for purposive dialogue, that is, conversation as a deliberate leadership tool in times of complexity. This framework identifies five key functions of leadership conversation. Each is more than just a technique; it's a strategic intervention aligned with a category of lived experience from Lens 1:

- **As Transmission**—Delivering direction, ensuring clarity and compliance
- **As Relationship**—Building trust, engagement, and psychological safety
- **As Sensemaking**—Helping others interpret complexity and change
- **As Alignment**—Linking individuals and actions to broader strategic purpose
- **As Transformation**—Reframing identities and opening new possibilities

Together, these functions demonstrate how leadership dialogue moves beyond exchange into strategic action. Each one connects back to the internal experiences captured by Lens 1, creating a dynamic link between a leader's awareness and their impact.

Lens 2: Conversation Functions

This next section introduces Lens 2 more formally and presents a practical framework for translating internal leadership awareness into intentional action. It addresses a key question: What is the purpose of a leadership conversation when change is unfolding?

Where Lens 1 revealed the leader's stance, mindset, and interpretive habits, Lens 2 highlights the strategic utility of conversation in uncertain environments. These conversation functions are not simply about improving communication; they are high-leverage interventions designed to influence how people make meaning, stay motivated, align with strategy, and shift perspectives.

This model positions the leader not only as a communicator but as a facilitator of movement, across ideas, relationships, systems, and identities. In moments where complexity might otherwise stall momentum, these five conversation functions offer a way forward.

The Five Functional Purposes of Leadership Conversation

With Lens 2, we move from reflective insight to strategic application. The framework introduced here identifies five core purposes of leadership conversation, each representing more than a style or tone. These are deliberate, functional uses of dialogue that support purposeful leadership action during change.

Each conversational function serves as a strategic intervention: a way of advancing the work, navigating complexity, and supporting people through transition. These are not rigid categories but instead adaptive modes of engagement that leaders can draw on, combine, or shift between, depending on the needs of the moment.

The five functions outlined below form the external action dimension of the Dual-Lens Framework. Each corresponds to a category of experience from Lens 1, linking internal awareness with external impact. In moments of ambiguity, disruption, or transformation, they offer a map for how leaders can use their words not just to respond but to lead.

Let's examine each function in turn:

1. **As Transmission—Strategically Intentional**
   Conversation is used to deliver information, directives, expectations, or strategic updates with clarity and control. It serves a functional, top-down purpose, often aimed at consistency or compliance.

   Example: A project sponsor briefs the team on updated compliance requirements from a regulatory body. The leader clearly outlines new documentation expectations, deadlines, and nonnegotiable standards to ensure legal and procedural alignment across all workstreams.

2. **As Relationship—Building Shared Commitment**
Conversation is used to build rapport, psychological safety, and trust. Leaders attend to emotional undercurrents and interpersonal dynamics, fostering belonging and shared ownership.

     Example: In a one-on-one with a team member who's feeling overwhelmed, the leader listens attentively, acknowledges the emotional load, and shares appreciation for the person's contribution. This conversation strengthens trust and fosters a sense of psychological safety within the project environment.

3. **As Sensemaking—Mindful Awareness**
Conversation is a reflective, inquiry-based process through which meaning is cocreated. Leaders and teams interpret ambiguous situations together, surfacing assumptions and navigating uncertainty.

     Example: After a stakeholder workshop reveals unexpected resistance, the project manager invites the team into a debrief conversation. They ask reflective questions to unpack assumptions, surface concerns, and coconstruct a shared understanding of what the pushback reveals about deeper organizational tensions.

4. **As Alignment/Transformation—Guiding the Change**
Conversation is both diagnostic and developmental. It aligns perspectives, integrates divergent views, and creates cohesion across roles and systems. This function consolidates prior modes into a harmonized, strategic outcome.

     Example: As the project approaches a critical integration milestone, the leader convenes cross-functional leads to clarify priorities, surface interdependencies, and codesign adjustments to the implementation roadmap. The dialogue aligns perspectives and recommits the group to shared outcomes.

5. **As Transformation—Catalyst for Change**
Conversation is leveraged to shift mindsets, inspire action, and catalyze transformation at both individual and organizational levels. It encourages reframing and reimagining what's possible.

Example: During a project kickoff, the leader shares a compelling vision of how the new system will not only streamline operations but also redefine how teams collaborate across departments. The conversation sparks energy and shifts team members' mindsets from skepticism to curiosity about the change.

The external strategic action dimension of Lens 2 (what leaders are trying to accomplish through conversation) is strongly supported by the contemporary research of Rizvi and Popli (2021) and Souza and Wood (2022). Rizvi and Popli (2021) argue that leadership communication goes beyond information transmission to become a vehicle for shaping team behavior and catalyzing transformation. Their work reinforces the idea that conversations function not only as expressions of leader identity but as intentional acts that influence how change is enacted and sustained. Similarly, Souza and Wood (2022) advocate for a multilens approach to leadership that operates across individual, relational, and collective levels. Their emphasis on adaptable, context-aware leadership affirms the need for structured conversations that serve systemic purposes.

Together, these studies validate Lens 2 as a practical framework for external, purposive dialogue, extending the strategic utility of leadership conversation in complex, people-centered change initiatives.

The Dual-Lens Framework brings together two essential dimensions of leadership: internal awareness and external impact. Lens 1, the categories of experience, reflects the leader's internal awareness, how they understand and engage in their conversations. Lens 2, the conversation functions, reveals the external strategic purpose of those conversations, what they are trying to achieve within the context of change.

When viewed together, each function corresponds to a particular way of experiencing leadership: Transmission aligns with strategic intent, Relationship with building shared commitment, Sensemaking with mindful awareness, Alignment with guiding collective action, and Transformation with catalyzing identity shifts. Effective change leadership requires fluency in both lenses: the self-reflective insight to understand one's own conversational posture, and the situational agility to meet the evolving needs of the team, moment, or mission.

If Chapter 1 asked us to rethink what leadership means in a project environment, this chapter asks us to practice it when the ground is shifting. Leading through the gray zone means navigating ambiguity, relational tension, and emotional undercurrents, those messy moments in a project or transformation initiative where no amount of planning seems to offer clarity. It is precisely in these spaces that reflective leadership becomes most necessary and most powerful.

The gray zone is not a detour; rather, it's part of the road. And yet, traditional leadership instincts often tell us to accelerate through it, to double down on control, efficiency, and resolution. But reflective leaders know something different: when we pause, get curious, and name what is unfolding beneath the surface, we find new ways forward. This chapter explores how to lead when the path ahead is unclear, using real examples, reflective tools, and the Dual-Lens Framework introduced in Chapter 1 and here. We will see how project, change, and executive leaders can use reflection not only to adapt but to transform the spaces they lead.

The Nature of the Gray Zone

The gray zone emerges when familiar markers disappear, when priorities are competing, clarity is missing, and relationships are strained. In transformation efforts, this space is unavoidable. A major shift in digital systems, for example, may reveal outdated workflows, unspoken hierarchies, or deep emotional attachments to legacy ways of working. These aren't just technical problems; they are cultural and relational puzzles.

Leaders often default to old habits in the face of uncertainty. They move faster, assert control, and frame ambiguity as a threat to overcome. But the gray zone is not inherently a problem; rather, it's a space of potential. It invites us to lead differently.

Reflective leadership in the gray zone begins by resisting urgency. It asks us to slow down long enough to sense what's really happening. What are people not saying? What assumptions are we holding? What is trying to emerge?

These are questions a checklist won't answer. This is where the Dual-Lens Framework becomes vital.

Applying the Dual-Lens Framework in Practice

The dual-lens framework pairs two ways of seeing leadership conversation:

- Experience categories: How leaders understand their conversations
- Conversation functions: The purpose the conversation serves in a change process

In the gray zone, leaders move fluidly (or get stuck) across these dimensions. A project leader may start with the intent to transmit updates but recognize the need to shift into a sensemaking mode. An executive might open a meeting with strategic alignment but need to move toward emotional transparency when resistance surfaces. Likewise, a change leader may begin with relationship-building to foster trust but find that reframing the narrative becomes essential to renew momentum and inspire commitment.

Consider how the five conversation functions interact with lived experience:

- Transmission/Strategically Intentional—"Here's what needs to happen."
- Relationship/Building Shared Commitment—"How are we experiencing this, together?"
- Sensemaking/Mindful Awareness—"What do you make of this?"
- Alignment/Guiding the Change—"How does this connect to our purpose?"
- Transformation/Catalyst for Change—"What might this invite us to become?"

Using this Dual-Lens Framework, reflective leaders can shift the shape and impact of their conversations in real time. They develop an awareness not only of what they're saying but why, and what the moment might call for instead.

In Practice: Reflective Leadership in the Gray Zone

Let's return to the Navigating the Gray Zone case study from Chapter 1 to see how reflection shifts the course of leadership.

A cross-departmental team was implementing a new intake process to streamline services and promote equity. The project had fallen behind schedule. Nia, the project lead, focused narrowly on deliverables. Marcus, the change strategist, was brought in to boost staff engagement but found himself pushing top-down messaging. Elena, the senior leader, felt mounting pressure from above and grew impatient with the pace of progress. A team meeting ended in visible frustration. Staff felt unheard. Managers disengaged. Misalignment and relational strain had overtaken the original intent of the initiative.

The three leaders regrouped. What began as a tactical debrief evolved into a reflective conversation. Each leader confronted uncomfortable truths: Nia realized she was hiding behind process to avoid emotional discomfort. Marcus acknowledged the unspoken power dynamics he had overlooked. Elena admitted that fear of failure had caused her to overcontrol.

This moment of reflection sparked a shift, not just in mindset but in how they would move forward together. Using the reflective worksheet introduced in Chapter 1, they processed the conversation through a dual-lens approach.

Nia—The Project Lead

- Observed Leadership Mindset: Defensive, rigid, focused on execution
- Lens 1 Category: Strategically Intentional—Focused on task delivery, resistant to emotional or relational dynamics
- Lens 2 Conversation Function: Transmission, with little space for dialogue
- Insight: Avoidance of relational work was harming team cohesion
- Action: Paused timelines, opened feedback loops. Asked, "What do we need to feel heard?"

Marcus—The Change Strategist

- Observed Leadership Mindset: Frustrated, disconnected from power realities
- Lens 1 Category: Mindful Awareness—Sensed deeper dynamics but lacked the influence or structure to shift them
- Lens 2 Conversation Function: Intended transformation, but defaulted to strategy without trust
- Insight: Emotional safety was missing. Without it, no strategy could land.
- Action: Shifted from presenting to sensemaking. Asked, "What's not being said in this room?"

Elena—The Executive Leader

- Observed Leadership Mindset: Anxious, controlling, focused on outcomes
- Lens 1 Category: Guiding the Change—Pressured to lead from the front, but missing collaborative cues
- Lens 2 Conversation Function: Aimed for alignment, came across as directive
- Insight: Pressure distorted her leadership presence
- Action: Named her fear with the team, modeled vulnerability, invited coleadership

Together, they reframed success—not just timelines met but trust rebuilt. They returned to their teams not with answers but with better questions. What emerged wasn't a smoother plan, but a more human-centered process that could adapt, connect, and grow.

This is the work of reflective leadership: to create space in the gray zone for sensemaking, trust-building, and emergence. It's not always fast. But it's what moves transformation from intent to impact.

Beyond the Case: Patterns of Reflective Leadership

The Gray Zone case is not unique. Across sectors, from public health to higher education to tech start-ups, leaders are encountering similar moments of uncertainty, complexity, and emotional weight. What differentiates successful transformation efforts isn't the absence of gray zones, but the presence of leaders willing to reflect inside them.

In a public health organization launching a new community care model, the project lead noticed a rise in passive resistance during team updates. Rather than escalate performance measures, she paused the process, invited frontline staff into conversation, and asked what was missing. The answer wasn't more training. It was clarity on purpose and voice in decision making. Reflection surfaced what metrics had masked.

In a university setting, a change leader overseeing an equity audit realized that her strategic messaging was being interpreted as criticism. After several strained sessions, she shifted her approach, acknowledging discomfort, slowing her pace, and inviting department heads to share their own equity stories. The result was not just buy-in but ownership.

And in a tech start-up, an executive under pressure to pivot after market changes found himself reverting to hyperproductivity and missed team burnout signals. A mentor asked, "What are you avoiding in your urgency?" That one question led to a full team reset, including mental health resources and a new cadence of reflective team check-ins.

What these stories reveal are patterns: Leaders paused before pushing forward. They named the emotional context, not just the technical one. They shifted from answers to questions. They chose dialogue over directive. Reflective leadership is not about having it all figured out. Rather, it's about creating space to figure it out together.

Barriers to Reflection

Even with the best of intentions, reflective leadership is often difficult to practice, especially in high-pressure, results-driven environments. Leaders face many internal and external barriers:

- Performance pressure: The expectation to "keep things moving" can discourage pausing.
- Organizational culture: Many workplaces still reward decisiveness over curiosity, and control over connection.
- Emotional discomfort: Reflecting requires vulnerability. For some, this feels risky or unfamiliar.

- Time scarcity: When resources are limited, leaders often cut the very practices that build resilience.

Despite these challenges, reflection is not a luxury; rather, it's a capacity-building necessity. To support leaders in identifying and working through their barriers, let me introduce the Reflection Readiness Scan.

Tool 2: Reflection Readiness Scan

This tool helps leaders recognize what may be getting in the way of reflection, and how to shift.

Step 1: Identify the Current State. Am I rushing decisions or skipping debriefs? When was the last time I asked, What are we learning? Do I avoid emotional or relational conversations?

Step 2: Notice Internal Signals. What's driving my pace: fear, pressure, proving myself? What emotions do I suppress in meetings? Where am I holding back from asking deeper questions?

Step 3: Choose One Practice to Reclaim Space. Schedule a 15-minute solo reflection after key meetings. Invite someone to name what they notice in your leadership style. Start one meeting a week with a reflective prompt.

This scan isn't about judgment, it's about self-awareness. The more leaders can name their barriers, the more intentional they can become in making space for meaningful, human-centered leadership.

Using the Dual-Lens Framework in Practice: A Leader's Guide to Adaptive Conversation

The Dual-Lens Framework equips leaders to navigate complex change by combining two perspectives:

- Conversation Experience Categories: How leaders experience and make meaning of their conversations
- Conversation Functions: The purpose each conversation serves within the flow of change

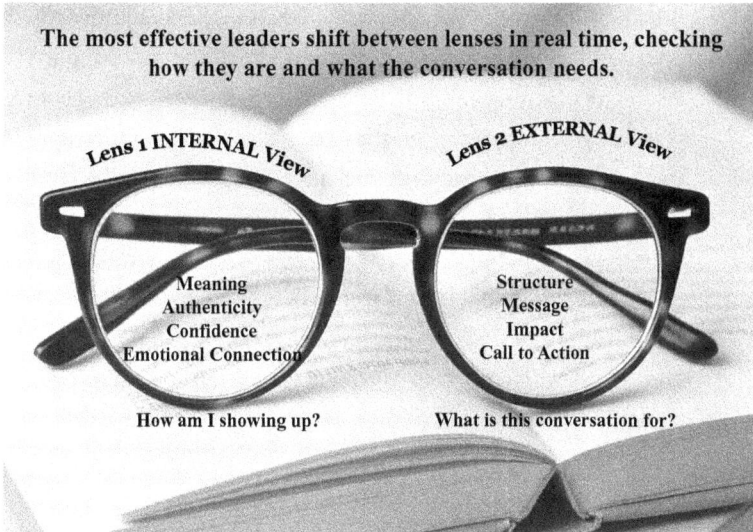

Figure 2.1 The Dual-Lens leadership check

When used together, these lenses help leaders shift their conversational approach in real time, based not just on what they want to say but what the moment calls for.

Figure 2.1 demonstrates how effective leaders move fluidly between the internal view (reflection, insight, learning, adaptability) and the external view (application, facilitation, strategy, measurable results). By asking, "How am I showing up?" and "What is this conversation for?" in real time, they align personal presence with purposeful action.

Contribution to Practice

The Dual-Lens framework offers a practical contribution to the evolving field of project and change leadership by equipping leaders with tools to act more reflectively and relationally in complex environments. Specifically, it provides:

- A vocabulary for self-reflection: Leaders gain language to describe the intentions, assumptions, and functions of their conversations. This helps them examine their own habits and assess whether their communication aligns with the needs of the moment.

- A map for designing intentional conversations: By linking conversation types to leadership outcomes, the framework supports deliberate planning and real-time adaptation. Leaders can choose, shape, and sequence conversations to foster clarity, connection, and commitment throughout a change process.
- A method for shifting style based on situational needs: Grounded in both phenomenographic research and practical application, the framework guides leaders to flex between transmission, relationship-building, sensemaking, alignment, and transformation, based on factors such as readiness, resistance, or turning points in a project.

This dual-lens focus, on introspective awareness and outward impact, continues to be validated by emerging research. Rizvi and Popli (2021) highlight the increasing importance of reflective competence in strategic leadership, while Souza and Wood (2022) emphasize the value of dialogic practice in achieving adaptive and participatory outcomes. Together, these findings support the relevance of a model that helps leaders think and lead through conversation, not just action.

The framework also aligns with broader shifts IN contemporary leadership thinking. Human-centered leadership frameworks now emphasize presence, empathy, and cocreation over command-and-control.

Disciplines such as conversational intelligence (Glaser 2016) and dialogic organization development (Bushe and Marshak 2015) stress the transformative role of conversation in shaping culture, unlocking innovation, and building trust in times of uncertainty. Denning (2020) adds that leadership communication must move beyond direction-giving to create shared understanding through narrative and ongoing dialogue, particularly in agile, change-driven environments. Similarly, Kools and Kearns (2022) argue that in today's complex systems, leadership dialogue is not merely a skill but a vital capacity for collective learning, adaptability, and systemic change. In this way, the Dual-Lens Framework bridges theory and practice. It supports leaders in becoming more responsive, relational, and resilient, starting with the way they talk, listen, and learn together.

Recognizing the Right Conversation Function

Different stages of change and varying team dynamics call for different kinds of conversations. A critical leadership skill, especially in times of uncertainty, is knowing which type of conversation to lead, and when. The effectiveness of a conversation hinges on both the needs of the moment and the readiness of the people involved.

Lens 2 helps leaders identify the strategic function of a conversation: Are you trying to inform, build trust, make sense of ambiguity, align priorities, or reframe possibilities? These five functions are not fixed steps; rather, they're responsive choices that depend on real-time cues like team energy, trust levels, and the phase of the project.

The guidance below helps leaders assess which function to prioritize based on:

- Team readiness
- Resistance or trust levels
- Critical transition points in a project

Case Example: Adapting Across Functions

To illustrate how leaders apply these functions in practice, the following case traces a real-world initiative across four key moments. Each scene shows how leaders adjusted their conversational approach to meet evolving needs within the same change initiative.

Context: A midsize nonprofit is rolling out a new client intake platform. The change involves technology, workflow redesign, and cultural shifts.

Key Roles:
- Arjun Rahman—Project Lead
- Luis Jarvis—Change Advisor
- Cassidy Winslow—Executive Sponsor

Scene 1: Kickoff Meeting
Team Readiness: High energy, but confusion about purpose
Function Used: **Transmission**

Arjun opens by clarifying deliverables and expectations: "Here's what's happening, when, and why."

Scene 2: Early Feedback Shows Frustration

Resistance Level: Staff are overwhelmed and disengaged.

Function Shifted To: **Sensemaking + Relationship**

Luis facilitates a reflective session:

"What are you hearing from your teams? What's unclear? What are people feeling but not saying?"

Scene 3: Conflict Between Departments

Trust and Alignment: Beginning to erode

Function Shifted To: **Transformation**

Cassidy meets with team leads:

"If this project succeeded, what might it change about how we work together? What would be possible that isn't today?"

Scene 4: Preparing for Organizationwide Launch

Transition Point: Scaling to the wider organization

Function Shifted To: **Alignment**

Arjun reconnects the work to broader strategy:

"Let's revisit how this connects to our mission and why it matters now."

Practical Integration for Leaders

To embed this practice into your daily leadership, consider the following:

- **Before** key conversations: Review the five conversation functions and choose with intention.
- **Afterward:** Debrief with your team or reflect independently, what function did that conversation serve? What was missing?
- **With your team:** Share the Dual-Lens framework so that others can recognize and request the kind of dialogue they need.

Bridging to Chapter 3: From Function to Reflection

So far, we've explored how conversations function strategically in change environments. But being intentional in the moment requires more than choosing the right function, it requires real-time self-awareness.

That's where reflection comes in.

The next chapter focuses on developing your reflective capacity as a leader. You'll learn how to pause, process, and apply insight, both before and after conversations. The next tool will help guide that process.

The **Conversation Reflection Compass** (Tool 3) is a practical reflection tool designed to help leaders pause and make sense of high-stakes or emotionally charged conversations. It bridges the leader's **internal experience (Lens 1)** with the **strategic function (Lens 2)** of the dialogue, guiding users through four concise but powerful reflection points.

Ideal for solo reflection, coaching sessions, or team debriefs, the Compass supports both real-time awareness and intentional action. It can be used before or after key conversations, especially during the gray zones of change, to align personal growth with collective impact. The tool encourages leaders to treat every conversation as a learning opportunity by asking:

- How did I show up?
- What was I trying to accomplish?
- What impact did it have?
- What could I adapt next time?

By connecting how conversations are experienced with what they are designed to achieve, the Conversation Reflection Compass (see Appendix B) strengthens a leader's ability to respond with clarity, empathy, and purpose.

Reflective Prompts

What function did this conversation serve: Transmission, Sensemaking, Relationship, Alignment, or Transformation, and was that the right choice for this moment?

Which type of conversation do you most naturally lead with? Which feels most underused in your leadership?

How might your team's experience of change shift if you experimented with a different conversational approach?

Learning Outcomes

The following outcomes summarize the knowledge and skills you've developed in this chapter:

- Describe the five conversation functions of Lens 2 and how each aligns with categories of experience from Lens 1.
- Assess which conversation function best fits a given change context, based on team readiness, trust levels, and project timing.
- Adapt your conversational approach in response to evolving dynamics within a project or change initiative.
- Use the Conversation Reflection Compass (Tool 3) to strengthen real-time awareness and post-conversation insight.

A Glimpse Ahead

As we've seen in this chapter, leading in the gray zone requires more than just technical competence; it calls for emotional insight, adaptive dialogue, and the courage to reflect in motion. The Dual-Lens Framework offers a way to navigate this complexity, helping leaders align their inner experience (Lens 1) with the strategic function of their conversations (Lens 2). When leaders are able to pause, reflect, and shift perspective, they open the door to more honest, human-centered, and transformational change.

In Chapter 3, we take that reflection deeper. We introduce reflective practice as a foundational leadership tool, not just for learning after the fact but for leading in real time. Grounded in adult learning theory, systems thinking, and lived experience, reflection becomes a form of leadership intelligence. You'll explore how mindfulness and sensemaking work together to build team resilience, surface insight, and cocreate new meaning. When leaders lead reflectively, they do not just respond to change but shape it.

"Leadership Reflection Break"

"Trying to get the crux of it and to the barriers. Sometimes we send mixed messages, there are so many priorities out there, and people are being told about all the priorities, all the barriers. We want people to develop; to develop the ability to see the path forward."

CHAPTER 3

Reflective Practice as a Leadership Discipline

Opening Scene: The Meeting Before The Meeting

It wasn't on the calendar, but in the unspoken exchanges, alignment was being tested and trust quietly negotiated.

Elena sat in her car, engine off, eyes fixed on the building ahead. The morning sun hadn't yet lifted the frost from the windows, and inside the glass atrium of WynnTech's headquarters, the hum of another leadership meeting awaited her. But she wasn't ready to walk in. Not yet.

She tightened her grip on her coffee mug, the warmth grounding her in the present moment. Her day was structured to the minute: quarterly reporting at 9:00, transformation status review at 10:30, and executive roundtable before noon. All part of the plan. But something inside her felt out of sync.

She glanced at the printed slide deck beside her: "Strategic Priorities for Q3." Every bullet point was technically accurate—streamlined processes, improved adoption, and cost-efficiency gains. Yet none of it captured what she had heard in the hallway yesterday. Frustration. Fatigue. Fear of irrelevance.

A week earlier, during a leadership feedback session Marcus had facilitated, a senior manager had said quietly:

"We're performing the change, but we're not feeling the change."

That comment hadn't left her. Elena had nodded along at the time, but the words lingered in her chest like static.

She exhaled slowly and leaned back, asking herself, "What was I missing?"

For years, she had equated executive presence with decisiveness, calm, and assertive clarity. But lately, she'd begun to suspect that something else was needed. Something softer. Slower. More open. She reached into her bag and pulled out the small navy notebook her business coach had given her. On the first page, she'd scribbled a question that had unsettled her ever since:

"What am I pretending not to notice?"

She tapped her pen against the page, then wrote a single word: Pace. Then another: Distance.

And finally, a phrase she didn't yet understand: Listening for meaning.

Inside, the meeting was about to start. But outside, in the quiet of her own awareness, a different kind of leadership was taking shape. One that didn't begin with answers, but with questions. Elena didn't know exactly how to bring that reflection into the room. But she knew she couldn't keep leading from the surface.

She pulled the key out of the ignition and whispered, "Let's try something different today."

Elena found herself rehearsing this difficult conversation in her head before the town hall. She had always relied on experience, but this time, the stakes felt different. She paused to journal, something she hadn't done in years. She started by writing what she planned to say, but ended by uncovering what she truly needed to understand. It was not the script; it was the story behind it.

As she sat alone in her office, the draft of her upcoming town hall remarks were open on her screen. She had revised the script four times and still, something about it felt hollow. The words hit all the right notes—vision, values, and performance—but they didn't reflect how she actually felt. Truthfully, she was anxious. The team was fatigued. And part of her was questioning the pace of the change she had once championed.

Instinctively, she opened her journal. At first, she copied over lines from her speech, but soon the words shifted.

"I'm afraid to tell them I don't have all the answers," she wrote. "I'm afraid that slowing down will be seen as weakness."

She sat with those admissions, letting the vulnerability settle. Then she turned a new page and wrote: "What if I spoke from here instead?"

That single reflective pause changed how she approached the town hall. She didn't abandon the plan, but she rewrote her opening, framing it around a story, her own discomfort, her learning, her hope. And when she delivered it, she noticed people leaning in, not because she was perfect but because she was real.

In a world of constant change, leadership is no longer defined solely by decision making or direction-setting. It is equally defined by sensemaking, self-awareness, and the ability to reflect in action and on action. This chapter introduces reflective practice as a core leadership discipline, one that enables individuals to pause, notice, and intentionally shape the conversations that define projects, teams, and transformation efforts.

Drawing from adult learning theory, we understand that leaders learn not just from experience but from interpreting that experience. Reflection transforms action into insight. From organizational systems thinking, we learn that what leaders pay attention to—what they name, question, or ignore—shapes the behavior and dynamics of the system. And from personal experience, we know that the best leadership moments often emerge not from control but from curiosity and connection.

This chapter lays the foundation for the Dual-Lens Framework by presenting five distinct categories of experience leaders may bring to their conversations, ranging from transactional exchanges to moments of transformation. If you recall, these categories are not personality types or rigid communication styles. They reflect evolving patterns of how leaders perceive and engage in conversation, shaped by context, self-awareness, and developmental maturity. Through the Dual-Lens Framework, leaders begin to see that how they experience a conversation (Lens 1) is inseparable from what they are trying to achieve (Lens 2).

For a project leader, this might mean noticing when urgency is driving directive communication, and intentionally shifting to sensemaking to reduce ambiguity. A change leader might recognize the need to move from analysis to shared storytelling to rebuild trust. An executive leader might pause a strategic update to lean into vulnerability and relational repair.

By becoming more aware of their own conversational stance, leaders unlock a fuller range of options, choosing dialogue over monologue, purpose over reaction, and transformation over habit. This is where reflective leadership begins to reshape culture, conversation by conversation.

At the heart of this shift is a simple truth:

Leadership conversations are mindful, a process of continually orienting, adjusting, and creating opportunities for deeper, more meaningful possibilities.

Why This Matters in the Dual-Lens Framework

Reflective practice aligns with Lens 1: Mindful Awareness and Lens 2: As Sensemaking. This chapter explores how reflection allows leaders to interpret experience, cultivate resilience, and cocreate meaning with teams. Instead of reacting instinctively, leaders who pause to reflect help teams make sense of ambiguity together.

The Leadership Gap: What the Data Shows

Despite increased attention to leadership development and communication strategies, many organizations continue to struggle with inconsistent messaging, misaligned priorities, and a perceived disconnect between leaders and their teams. Employees often feel unheard, underinformed, or overwhelmed during times of change, leading to erosion in trust. This continued lack of trust in leadership has significant implications for leadership dialogue.

When trust is low, even well-intended conversations may be met with skepticism, resistance, or disengagement. Leaders must recognize that dialogue is not merely a vehicle for communication but a foundational tool for trust-building. High-trust environments require more than clarity; they demand authentic, relational, and sensemaking-focused conversations that invite transparency, vulnerability, and shared ownership. The Dual-Lens Framework becomes especially valuable in this context, equipping leaders to match the internal experience of dialogue (Lens 1) with the external function (Lens 2) to rebuild connection, alignment, and belief in the leadership journey.

In a recent study, McKinsey (2023) emphasized that even well-planned transformation initiatives often fail when "the change story is unclear or uninspiring." Even well-conceived transformation initiatives can falter when the change narrative is unclear, misaligned, or uninspiring. This McKinsey research highlights that large-scale efforts, such as those involving generative AI, often stall not due to poor strategy but because the vision isn't meaningfully translated across the organization. Without a compelling and credible story, change fails to take root at scale.

This underscores a critical truth: Narrative isn't a side element of change; it is core leadership work. Dialogue becomes the vehicle through which leaders clarify intent, interpret complexity, and invite commitment. Through the Dual-Lens Framework, leaders can assess not just what story they're telling (Lens 2: purpose) but how they're showing up in the telling (Lens 1: experience), ensuring the message resonates and mobilizes action.

People don't just need to know what to do. They need to know why it matters. And they need to hear that story from someone they trust.

Why Story Works: A Neuroscience Perspective

Narrative is not just emotional but also neurological. Research in cognitive psychology and neuroscience shows that stories activate parts of the brain associated with empathy and memory more effectively than facts or bullet points alone (Zak 2018). When leaders tell stories, listeners are more likely to:

- Retain the message.
- Feel connected to the speaker.
- Apply the message to their own context.
- In short: Facts inform, but stories move people.

Storytelling as a Strategic Tool

Storytelling isn't only for TED Talks or branding campaigns. In leadership, story is a sensemaking device, a way to make complexity coherent, and ambiguity navigable. According to Karl Weick (2001), sensemaking is central to how people adapt to change. Stories help people:

- Simplify chaos without erasing it
- See themselves in a broader context
- Engage emotionally with rational decisions

A strong leadership story:

- Names the change or challenge
- Connects it to values and purpose
- Offers a narrative arc of possibility
- Invites listeners to participate in the next chapter

What employees and stakeholders need in moments of uncertainty is a compelling, credible story, one that helps them see why change is happening, where they fit, and what the future could look like. The following integration activities help embed that story into team culture, communication, and action:

- Journaling on how recent conversations fall into different categories or functions
- Using the Dual-Lens Framework to track the evolution of team conversations over a project life cycle

Reflective Prompts

When did I last invite others to make sense of change with me? How can I bring more of that into my next leadership moment?

Reflection Through the Dual-Lens Framework

The Dual-Lens Framework introduced in Chapters 1 and 2 invites leaders to examine both the internal experience and the external function of their conversations. Reflection acts as the connective tissue between these two dimensions.

On the experience side, reflective practice helps leaders notice their inner drivers: fear of conflict, the desire to appear competent, or discomfort with uncertainty. At WynnTech, Elena's self-awareness about her tendency to control meetings surfaced only through journaling, an experience lens moment.

On the function side, reflection sharpens how leaders shape outcomes. Nia, known for her precise execution, realized her updates were landing more as directives than dialogue. Through reflective prompts embedded into her team meetings, she began asking questions that shifted the purpose of the conversation, from transmission to cocreation.

Marcus learned that his carefully structured transformation updates were missing emotional resonance. He reflected on why people weren't responding, and realized he was leading with logic but avoiding vulnerability. Over time, his functional goal evolved: from "explain the plan" to "invite meaning-making."

In both lenses, reflection slows leaders down, not to reduce momentum, but to increase alignment. It reveals where intention and impact diverge. And it opens up new possibilities for leading conversations that matter.

From Individual to Collective Reflection

Reflective practice often begins with personal insight, but its greatest power is unleashed when embedded across teams and systems. At WynnTech, the reflective shift followed a natural progression:

Individual: Elena's journaling practice became a touchstone for her leadership. She used prompts like, "What surprised me today?" and "Where did I lead from fear?" to ground her awareness before making decisions.

Team: Nia's team began regular "sensemaking sessions" where they reflected not just on what happened but how the team felt during moments of success or failure. Trust deepened. Performance improved, not from pressure but from shared ownership.

Organization: Marcus initiated a "Pause Practice" at the portfolio level, encouraging teams to carve out 30 minutes biweekly to reflect on their dynamics and patterns. Leaders were invited to share these reflections across teams, surfacing systemic insights.

This multilevel approach reframed reflection as both a learning tool and a cultural lever. It signaled that inquiry was as valuable as execution, and that growth was everyone's responsibility.

Approaches to Daily Habits

Several approaches can support leaders in building a habit of reflection, each suited to different time constraints and emotional demands:

- **Gibbs's Reflective Cycle (1988):**
  Commonly used in health care and education, this structured framework guides users through six stages: Description, Feelings, Evaluation, Analysis, Conclusion, and Action Plan. Elena found this especially useful during emotionally charged stakeholder meetings, helping her unpack discomfort and realign her approach with clarity and intention.
- **Reflection in 5 Minutes:**
  For time-pressed leaders, this simple framework includes three quick prompts:
  2. What did I notice?
  3. What felt off?
  4. What might I try next time?
     WynnTech leaders used this format in debriefs and coaching conversations to spark insight without adding complexity.
- **Digital Tools:**
  Some teams integrated reflection into their daily workflows, using journaling apps, voice memos, or tagging tasks in tools like Asana and Trello with "Reflection Required" to pause and learn from action.

When used consistently, these approaches normalize reflection as part of the work, not as a compliance task but as a strategic advantage in complex, evolving environments.

WynnTech Case: The Courage to Pause

The Q3 delivery cycle at WynnTech was rocky, scope shifts, timeline compressions, and competing executive narratives. At the post-cycle debrief, Elena noticed the team's reluctance to speak.

She took a breath, closed her laptop, and said, "Let's take a moment. What are we carrying that hasn't been said?"

Silence followed. Then Thomas, usually quiet, said, "I don't think we've acknowledged how hard this was."

Heads nodded. No blame surfaced, just weariness, and then relief. Elena held the space.

This moment wasn't in the plan. But it changed how the team approached the next cycle. They began naming their pressures earlier, offering support more freely, and scheduling midpoint check-ins to surface what wasn't obvious.

It started with a pause. And a question.

Grounding Practice: Perspectives from Leadership Literature

Reflective leadership is supported by a deep bench of theory and research. Argyris and Schön's (1974) concepts of single-loop and double-loop learning remind us that many leaders only reflect on outcomes, not on assumptions. At WynnTech, double-loop learning became critical as Marcus began to challenge the belief that stakeholder silence meant agreement.

Jennifer Garvey Berger's (2019) work on complexity leadership shows how reflection interrupts reactive habits. Her concept of "mind traps" aligns with Nia's realization that expertise can limit curiosity.

Brené Brown's (2018) research highlights how vulnerability is foundational to trust. Elena's openness in leadership meetings gave others permission to be real, not just right.

Edgar Schein's (2013) "humble inquiry" reinforces that the best leaders ask before they act. His work informed the redesign of WynnTech's project intake process, ensuring reflection happened before scope and timelines were locked.

Finally, David Rock's (2008) SCARF model provided language for the emotional dynamics at play: status, certainty, autonomy, relatedness, and fairness. Reflection helped leaders spot these cues and respond with care.

These scholars offer more than insight. They offer permission, to slow down, to question, to feel, and to grow.

Prompts and Practice Points

To close this chapter, consider incorporating the following reflective habits into your leadership rhythm:

Personal Prompts: What emotion is present for me right now? What assumptions am I carrying? Where am I avoiding feedback?

Team Prompts: What surprised us this week? What's not being said? Where are we aligned and where are we pretending to be?

Practice Points: Begin meetings with a moment of pause. Invite reflection into performance reviews. Create rituals of closure and transition after major deliverables.

Reflective Prompts

When was the last time you paused to consider not just what went wrong (or right) in a project but why it happened that way?

Consider a recent project or leadership moment you've reflected on. Whose voice or perspective did you not include in that reflection? What might they have seen that you didn't?

Learning Outcomes

The following outcomes summarize the knowledge and skills you've developed in this chapter:

- Define "gray zones" in organizational change and explain why they require fluid movement between the two lenses.
- Diagnose when a conversation is stuck in one function and how to shift it toward greater alignment or transformation.

- Integrate practical prompts to choose the right conversation function in high-stakes or uncertain moments.
- Anticipate and address resistance by balancing task focus with relationship and meaning-making.

A Glimpse Ahead

Reflection is where transformation begins, but it is not where it ends. Insight without dialogue stays private. Chapter 3 explored how leaders experience and interpret conversations; now we turn outward. As we move into Chapter 4, remember, reflection alone does not transform an organization. But it prepares the ground. The next step is conversation, the kind that moves people, bridges understanding, and aligns intention with action. Chapter 4 explores how dialogue becomes a driver of change. You'll discover how purposeful conversation, anchored in awareness (Lens 1) and guided by strategic function (Lens 2), can catalyze insight, build commitment, and turn reflection into momentum.

"Leadership Reflection Break"

"Before I go out into these face-to-face sessions, I conduct a bit of conversational research. I want to understand what is going on, I want to hear more, talk with my counterparts first and talk to my directs and then just listen and probe a bit."

CHAPTER 4

Dialogue That Drives Change

Opening Scene: The Question No One Expected

The room froze for just a second, long enough for an honest question to shift the conversation from updates to transformation.

Marcus stood at the head of the conference table, eyes scanning the tense faces of his colleagues. The project milestone had been missed, again, and the usual blame narrative was beginning to take shape. He felt the familiar urge to take control, to reassert authority and push through a plan. But something stopped him. Elena's words from last week echoed in his mind: "Sometimes the bravest thing a leader can do is pause long enough to let the real conversation emerge."

He took a breath, closed his laptop, and asked: "Before we talk about deliverables, what do you need right now to move forward?"

Silence.

Then Nia spoke. "I need clarity, on what matters most. Everything feels critical, and it's exhausting."

A few others nodded. Someone exhaled audibly.

The conversation that followed wasn't comfortable, but it was real. Instead of defensiveness, there was reflection. Instead of status reports, there was support. Marcus said less and listened more. In the quiet after the meeting, he typed on his tablet: "Dialogue shifted everything. Not the plan, but the people."

Later, in a hallway debrief with Elena and Nia, the group reflected on what had happened. "That question," Elena said, "changed the energy in the room. It invited truth."

That truth, not certainty, became the new starting point.

Marcus had felt the tension rise before he spoke, and part of him feared losing control of the room. But choosing curiosity over command shifted the atmosphere. "It was like opening a window," Nia said afterward. "We didn't realize how stifled it had become in there." For Marcus, it was a turning point, not just for the project but for his leadership.

He recalled similar moments during his earlier career, times he wished he had paused to ask rather than to push. This time, he had. And what emerged was not only a better conversation but a better sense of who his team was becoming.

This chapter moves beyond basic communication to explore leadership dialogue as a strategic lever for change. It introduces practical tools and conversational techniques that help leaders shift from transactional exchanges to transformational moments, where inquiry, deep listening, and purposeful framing build connection and clarity. While well-structured plans and change frameworks are essential, they are not sufficient. Many transformations stall not because of poor strategy but because dialogue breaks down. People resist not simply due to disagreement but because they don't feel seen, heard, or invited into the process. At the heart of successful change is the ability to converse meaningfully.

Using the Dual-Lens Framework, this chapter shows how leaders can move fluidly across the spectrum of conversation experiences and functions, from Strategically Intentional to Guiding the Change (Lens 1) and from Transmission to Transformation (Lens 2). Dialogue becomes more than a communication method, it becomes a practice of leadership.

Too often, organizations default to monologue during change: scripted updates, one-way announcements, and top-down messaging. These may inform, but they rarely inspire. What's needed is conversation that creates, not just disseminates, meaning.

"Dialogue is about turning the monologue of change into a shared language of possibility."

Why Dialogue Matters in Change Leadership

In times of change, leaders are expected to have answers. Yet the most powerful leadership conversations don't resolve ambiguity; rather, they create space within it. Dialogue, in this context, isn't just back-and-forth talk. It's a way of leading that values curiosity, connection, and cocreation.

Leadership theories have long recognized the importance of effective communication. But newer approaches, such as conversational intelligence (Glaser 2016), dialogic organization development (Bushe and Marshak 2015), and systemic leadership (Kools and Kearns 2022), extend that idea by framing dialogue as a tool for meaning-making. These approaches challenge the leader-as-expert model and emphasize the role of shared inquiry and learning in complex, adaptive systems.

Consider how many change efforts fail not because of poor strategy but because of poor conversation. People don't resist change as much as they resist feeling unheard or devalued. Dialogue changes that by offering space for involvement, for emotional integration, and for perspective-taking. It slows down the rush to action just enough to ask: What's really going on here?

Dialogue also plays a critical role in collective learning. Leaders who model openness, curiosity, and listening signal that it's safe to explore and experiment. When dialogue becomes part of the team's fabric, learning accelerates, even in the midst of uncertainty. As Denning (2020) notes, in agile environments, leaders who foster ongoing dialogue enable alignment, adaptation, and trust.

In short, when leaders use dialogue intentionally, they do not just manage change but also shape the context in which change becomes possible.

One powerful example comes from Satya Nadella, CEO of Microsoft (Humans of Globe 2024), who transformed the company's culture by shifting how leaders engaged in dialogue. Early in his tenure, Nadella encouraged leaders to move from a "know-it-all" to a "learn-it-all" mindset. This wasn't just a slogan, it became a behavioral shift in meetings, team reviews, and strategy sessions. Leaders were expected to ask questions, listen deeply, and remain open to challenge. Over time, this approach helped dismantle silos and sparked a culture of curiosity and collaboration.

Microsoft's cultural turnaround was not driven solely by strategy, but by dialogue, intentional, reflective, and inclusive.

Conversational Moves That Constrain Versus Create

In the heat of pressure, it's easy for leaders to default to patterns that constrain conversation. These include interrupting, defending, dismissing discomfort, or steering too quickly toward resolution. While often well intended, these moves close down inquiry and reinforce hierarchy.

Let's explore some of these common patterns:

Constraining Moves:

- Interrupting: Cutting someone off sends a message that speed matters more than substance.
- Defending a decision: Instead of exploring different views, this move shuts down debate and narrows focus.
- Dismissing discomfort: Phrases like, "Let's not get into that now" can invalidate lived experiences.
- Jumping to solutions: While efficient, it can cut short discovery and nuance.

Creating Moves:

- Pausing: Holding space shows that reflection is valued.
- Asking open-ended questions: Invites broader perspectives.
- Reflecting back: Validates the speaker's view, even if the leader doesn't agree.
- Naming tensions: Builds trust through authenticity.

Consider this exchange: "This isn't the time for blame." (Constraining) versus "It sounds like there's frustration here; can we explore what's underneath it?" (Creating)

These subtle differences have powerful effects. At WynnTech, Elena shifted from directing to inviting. In doing so, her team started surfacing issues earlier, and solving them faster.

Recognizing Your Default Moves:

- Take a moment to reflect on a recent conversation. Did you interrupt, reframe, defend, or stay silent? What would a creating move have looked like instead?

Techniques for Dialogue That Drives Change

Change-centered dialogue involves more than being a "good communicator." It's a skillful practice that blends listening, reflection, facilitation, and emotional intelligence. The techniques shared below are grounded in best practices and are widely used by organizations and change leaders to build momentum, reduce resistance, and foster engagement during times of transition. These approaches can be adapted across industries and leadership levels to support more effective and human-centered dialogue.

Appreciative Inquiry

Appreciative Inquiry focuses on strengths and what's working. For example, rather than asking, "Why did we miss the target?" A leader might ask, "What worked well during this phase, and how can we build on it?" At WynnTech, Marcus opened a retrospective with, "What surprised you, in a good way?" and saw new patterns emerge.

A Deeper Look: Appreciative Inquiry in Action

When the IT division at a large public health agency faced declining morale after a failed platform rollout, the new CIO introduced a teamwide appreciative inquiry session instead of a traditional root-cause analysis. The session began with small-group storytelling: "Tell us about a time during this project when you felt most engaged or proud of your work."

Surprisingly, even amid failure, teams shared moments of innovation, collaboration, and unexpected support. These stories reframed how they saw the project, and each other. The next step involved collectively identifying themes from the positive moments, which became the foundation for new team agreements and a redefined implementation strategy. What emerged wasn't denial of the failure, but a shift in energy from blame to belief in shared capability. Appreciative inquiry, in this context, helped the team reconnect to purpose and possibility, critical drivers in times of change.

Reframing

Reframing helps people see issues differently. Elena often used this during tense moments: "What might this challenge be teaching us?" Shifting the frame can release people from stuck narratives.

A Closer Look: Reframing in Action

During a portfolio review, a team at a midsize consulting firm expressed disappointment over the cancellation of a long-term client contract. The project lead was concerned about morale and began the meeting by acknowledging the loss. Then, she asked, "What might this pause create space for?" The team hesitated but gradually identified opportunities: investing time in professional development, improving internal processes, and dedicating energy to an emerging partnership. The shift reframed the event from failure to pivot. What had felt like a dead end became an inflection point.

Reframing helped the team recontextualize a setback, transforming energy from disappointment into strategic momentum.

Sensemaking Conversations

Sensemaking conversations are especially valuable during high ambiguity. When Nia's team received conflicting directives from different business units, she used visual mapping to untangle them together. This not only clarified confusion but created shared ownership.

A Closer Look: Sensemaking in Action

At a government agency undergoing structural reform, multiple departments received conflicting directives about how their roles would shift.

Frustration and confusion spread quickly. To address this, the change lead organized a sensemaking session.

He used a whiteboard to map out what was known, what was unclear, and what questions were emerging. People added sticky notes with their perspectives. The process didn't deliver answers, but it clarified shared uncertainties and helped normalize ambiguity.

The act of making sense together, openly and iteratively, relieved anxiety and built a sense of solidarity. People left feeling more grounded and engaged, even without a concrete resolution.

Narrative Reauthoring

This approach invites teams to rewrite the stories they tell about their work. After several months of delay and tension, Marcus invited his team to name their own turning point. They began describing themselves not as "behind" but as "building resilience." That subtle shift influenced tone, motivation, and confidence.

A Closer Look: Narrative Reauthoring in Action

In a global NGO, a regional team had internalized the story that they were always "the last to know," feeling overlooked and excluded from core decision making. This belief was undermining morale.

A new director asked each team member to briefly write the story of a moment when they influenced an outcome, no matter how small. In a facilitated workshop, these stories were shared, grouped, and reflected back as themes. The team began to see evidence of their agency and contribution.

This narrative reauthoring process did not erase their past frustrations, but it expanded their identity from "overlooked" to "capable of impact." That new narrative gave rise to renewed confidence and participation.

Intentional Pausing

Leaders like Elena model the pause. When tempers flared, she would simply say, "Let's take a breath before we continue." This disrupted reactivity and reset the emotional tone.

A Closer Look: Intentional Pausing in Action

During a high-stakes stakeholder meeting, a project manager was challenged on a recent decision. The tension in the room escalated. Instead of defending his position immediately, he paused, took a breath, and said, "I want to take a moment before I respond, because this matters."

That brief silence changed the room. It allowed emotions to settle and demonstrated his commitment to presence and thoughtfulness. He then responded with greater clarity and less defensiveness. Intentional pausing isn't just about silence, it's about reclaiming space for reflection and intention in the moment. When used well, it signals respect and emotional maturity.

Dialogic Tools

Leaders might also use practices like Dialogue Mapping, World Café, or liberating structures to facilitate group conversations. These frameworks help distribute voice and bring complexity to the surface in ways that are respectful and generative. Dialogic tools give leaders practical ways to surface complexity, invite diverse perspectives, and foster shared understanding, especially in large or cross-functional groups. Below are two widely used approaches.

A Closer Look: Dialogic Tools in Action

1. **Dialogue Mapping**

   Dialogue Mapping is a visual facilitation method that captures the flow of ideas, questions, concerns, and arguments during a conversation. It helps participants see how issues are connected, where consensus exists, and where differences remain. A facilitator uses a shared screen or whiteboard to map inputs in real time. For example, use a structured way to record a group discussion. In essence you are creating a conversation map, starting with a question, listing possible answers and adding reasons for and against each answer.

Use Case:

At a financial services firm undergoing a digital transformation, a team was divided on priorities for customer experience enhancements. Instead of debating in playback sessions, the leader used dialogue mapping to chart out each concern ("security," "usability," "cost efficiency") and how they linked to one another. This not only diffused defensiveness but allowed the group to spot a shared principle that ultimately guided their next iteration: "simplicity with trust."

2. **World Café**

   World Café is a structured conversational process that allows participants to discuss a question in small rotating groups. After several rounds, insights are harvested in a plenary session. This method emphasizes informal conversation and cross-pollination of ideas.

   Use Case:

   At WynnTech, Elena hosted a World Café to engage the extended project community in rethinking internal knowledge sharing. Over three rounds, participants rotated tables to discuss prompts such as, "What does meaningful collaboration look like here?" and "What barriers to sharing are unspoken?" The format gave voice to quieter team members, uncovered cultural blind spots, and produced themes that informed a new cross-team knowledge hub.

   The Impact:

   These tools democratize voice, surface tacit knowledge, and create a space where complexity is seen not as a problem to simplify but as a reality to embrace and explore. Leaders who use dialogic tools send a clear signal: Every perspective matters, and leadership is a shared act of learning. Together, these tools support not only change adoption but team cohesion, psychological safety, and adaptive capacity.

Power, Voice, and Inclusion in Dialogue

Dialogue that drives change must include those impacted by change. Too often, decisions are made without the voices of those most affected. Inclusion means bringing a wider range of perspectives into the conversation, and doing so in a way that honors their value.

At WynnTech, Marcus initially held closed-door meetings with senior stakeholders. The result? Mistrust from operational teams who felt overlooked. When he shifted to inviting cross-functional representatives, including junior staff, the tone changed. People felt heard. They became more invested.

Inclusion also means recognizing power dynamics. Who speaks first? Who gets credit for an idea? Who remains silent? Elena began experimenting with "first word from the quietest voice" in meetings. It was awkward at first, but it surfaced fresh insight and created new norms.

Research by Kools and Kearns (2022) suggests that dialogue across hierarchical levels enhances systemic intelligence. It allows learning and insight to flow both ways. In this sense, inclusion is not just a value but also a strategy.

Voice equity isn't about everyone speaking equally. It's about everyone having meaningful access to speak when it matters. Leaders must notice who's missing from the conversation, and actively invite them in.

Conversation Function Audit and Lens Integration

The Conversation Function Audit (Tool 4) helps leaders step back and ask: What purpose are my conversations serving? It draws on the five core conversation functions outlined in Lens 2:

- Transmission—Delivering information, giving instructions
- Relationship—Building connection, fostering trust
- Sensemaking—Interpreting meaning, creating shared understanding
- Alignment—Linking individual efforts to broader goals
- Transformation—Shifting mindset, expanding identity

Let's take a look at Marcus's week. Reviewing his calendar, he found that most conversations were task-focused: status updates, approvals, check-ins. Predominantly Transmission. While necessary, they weren't enough. So he began experimenting, opening one meeting a week with a question designed to invite Sensemaking or Alignment.

Elena used the Audit retroactively. After a tense stakeholder meeting, she asked herself: What function did that conversation serve? She realized she'd aimed for Alignment but defaulted to Transmission. The insight helped her prepare differently for the next conversation.

To integrate this into your practice:

Before a meeting: Ask, "What function do I want this conversation to serve?"

Afterward: Reflect, "What function did it actually serve?"

To further support leaders, a simple template can be used. Leaders can locate the Conversation Function Audit (Tool 4) in Appendix C. This tool enables leaders to align intent with impact and encourages ongoing reflection around how dialogue is used to serve people and purpose. Over time, map your dominant conversation types and adjust accordingly. Used consistently, the Audit helps leaders become more intentional, more flexible, and more attuned to what people, and systems, actually need.

Aligning Dialogue with the Dual-Lens Framework

This chapter's focus on conversation directly supports the Dual-Lens Framework for strategic change and project leadership implementations. While Lens 1 explores how leaders experience and make sense of conversation (from passive observer to transformative sense-maker), Lens 2 brings intentionality to what conversations are meant to accomplish.

Let's consider how these lenses work together.

A leader operating primarily in Lens 1 might reflect on how they showed up in a difficult team meeting, Did I speak too soon? Did I really listen? In Lens 2, the same leader adds a layer of intentionality. What was the function of that meeting? Did I aim to build alignment and end up defaulting to transmission?

The integration of both lenses encourages leaders to shift from reactive communicators to reflective change agents. For example, Elena's evolution at WynnTech, from directing team members to inviting generative dialogue, reflects movement through both lenses. She becomes more aware of how her leadership shows up in conversation (Lens 1) and more strategic in shaping the purpose and outcome of those conversations (Lens 2).

In practice, this integration means slowing down enough to ask not just, "What am I saying?" but, "What is this conversation for?" It means aligning how we speak with what we seek, to build trust, surface insight, and move people and systems forward.

Reflective Prompts

Dialogue isn't just something leaders do, it's how they lead. In complex change, it becomes the medium through which trust is built, assumptions are tested, and transformation takes root.

Let's end this chapter with some questions for your own reflection:

- Which conversational moves do you default to under pressure?
- When was the last time you invited a voice you normally overlook?
- What types of conversation are missing from your leadership practice?
- What function do you want your next critical conversation to serve?

"Change begins with conversation. And conversation begins with presence, courage, and curiosity."

Learning Outcomes

The following outcomes summarize the knowledge and skills you've developed in this chapter:

- Apply best-practice dialogue techniques such as Appreciative Inquiry, generative questioning, and active listening to change contexts.
- Differentiate between conversations that transmit information and those that foster shared meaning and ownership.
- Use dialogue to surface unspoken concerns, uncover interdependencies, and strengthen team trust.
- Facilitate conversations that integrate multiple perspectives without losing clarity or direction.

A Glimpse Ahead

Dialogue creates the conditions for change, it opens space for reflection, surfaces hidden concerns, and builds relational trust. But it is through story that leaders create coherence and momentum. Where dialogue invites shared understanding, storytelling weaves those insights into a compelling narrative that helps people move forward with purpose.

In Chapter 5, we shift from dialogue to storytelling, a deeply human and strategic leadership practice. You'll explore how stories create meaning, shape identity, and mobilize people toward change. Through story, not only do leaders just explain what is happening, but they also inspire what is possible. Building on the Dual-Lens Framework, this next chapter shows how narrative becomes a powerful bridge between what people experience (Lens 1) and what leaders intend to create (Lens 2). It is through story that leaders align the technical with the human, the strategy with the soul.

"Leadership Reflection Break"

"My conversations are spent coaching; a lot of time coaching and that is a very effective way of bringing the team together and moving ahead. I use this to draw them on board, participate and understand the big picture."

CHAPTER 5

Building Narrative Capacity in Project Teams

Opening Scene: Replaying the Story to See What's Missing

Looking back, it wasn't the metrics that revealed the truth, it was the gaps in their shared narrative that signaled where trust and clarity were needed.

Elena watched as the team settled into the informal semicircle they had arranged with comfortable chairs and coffee cups. It had been a long week, ten-hour days, several key deliverables behind schedule, and unresolved tension between engineering and operations. The usual approach would be a corrective stand-up or strategy reset. But today, she tried something different.

"Let's pause," she said. "No slides. No dashboards. I want to know where you are in your own story right now, this week, this sprint, this season."

The room was still at first, then someone said: "Honestly? I'm at the part where the hero's alone in the woods, not sure which way to go."

Chuckles followed. Another voice chimed in: "I think I'm at the unexpected mentor chapter. I had a one-on-one that shifted something."

What emerged over the next 40 minutes wasn't a project update; rather, it was a tapestry of human experiences, disappointments, small wins, and renewed resolve. Elena didn't have to manage energy. The playback session did that for her. Later that week, she jotted a reflection in her notebook: "Narrative isn't a tool for the end of the project. It's how we find meaning as we go."

This chapter explores how teams coauthor meaning through project storytelling. As initiatives evolve, the stories teams tell, about purpose, progress, and challenge, become a mirror of culture and a compass for direction. Building narrative capacity is not just about crafting messages but also about enabling teams to reflect, adapt, and reframe their own experience in real time.

Drawing on the Dual-Lens Framework, this chapter reflects the intersection of **Lens 1: Building Shared Commitment and Lens 2: Conversation as Relationship and Sensemaking**. It introduces practical techniques to help leaders embed storytelling and structured reflection into the everyday rhythms of team life, turning narrative into a leadership capability.

One key tool introduced here by Elena is the **Leadership Narrative Playback**, a structured storytelling practice that helps teams revisit and interpret the unfolding story of a project or change initiative. Rather than focusing solely on outcomes, Narrative Playback invites reflection on pivotal moments, shifts in identity, and the emotional undercurrents that shaped the journey. It helps surface meaning, strengthen cohesion, and align team perspectives around what matters most. Used consistently, this tool reinforces both awareness (how stories are received) and intentionality (what stories are meant to do), anchoring narrative as a core leadership function.

"Teams that can reflect together, grow together."

Tool 5: The Leadership Narrative Playback

This structured storytelling practice invites leaders and teams to reflect on recent experiences by "playing back" the narratives that emerged during a project, initiative, or change effort. Unlike a traditional debrief focused on performance metrics, Narrative Playback emphasizes meaning-making:

- What stories were told?
- What moments shaped identity or shifted momentum?
- Whose perspectives were amplified, or overlooked?

It can be used during retrospectives, transition milestones, leadership development sessions, or team reflections following high-stakes events. Narrative Playback is especially effective when:

- A project has shifted direction or purpose midstream.
- A change initiative is struggling with emotional undercurrents or misalignment.
- Teams are preparing for handoffs or renewal phases.
- There's a need to reconnect purpose, identity, and values across stakeholders.

Narrative Playback questions include:

- What was the story arc of this project or change?
- What moment changed how we saw ourselves?
- What meaning did different stakeholders take away?
- How can we carry the story forward with purpose?

This tool helps leaders shape not only individual insight, but also shared organizational memory. It aligns with the Dual-Lens Framework, helping leaders recognize both how stories are received (Lens 1: Experience) and what they are meant to achieve (Lens 2: Function). Used consistently, Leadership Narrative Playback surfaces blind spots, reinforces alignment, and enables teams to evolve toward more inclusive, strategic, and transformational narratives, building a leadership culture that listens, learns, and adapts through story.

When leaders engage in practices like Narrative Playback, they're doing more than reflecting on events; they're actively developing narrative capacity: the ability to construct, interpret, and communicate meaningful stories that align identity, strategy, and change. This capacity becomes essential in complex environments where facts alone are not enough; leaders must make meaning.

What Is Narrative Capacity?

Narrative capacity is the ability of a group to make sense of their collective experience by constructing, sharing, and evolving stories. It goes beyond storytelling as a communication tactic. In change leadership, narrative capacity is a strategic capability.

In projects, this capacity allows teams to situate their work within a larger purpose, interpret setbacks through learning lenses, and reframe challenges in real time. It also allows people to integrate their personal experiences into the collective meaning-making of a team or initiative.

As narrative capacity strengthens, so too does the organization's ability to shape and share a coherent identity. Leaders aren't just telling stories; they're influencing how people see themselves within the story of the team or organization. This is where narrative identity emerges. At the team and organizational level, narrative identity reflects the shared sense of who we are, how we got here, and what we're capable of becoming. It's built through patterns of conversation, symbolic moments, and repeated messages, and it profoundly impacts culture, engagement, and alignment during change.

Narrative Identity at the Team and Organizational Level

Just as individuals develop narrative identities, a sense of self shaped by the stories they tell and are told, teams and organizations also form shared narratives that shape how they see themselves, make decisions, and respond to challenge.

These collective stories are rarely written down, but they are deeply influential. Consider these examples:

- A project team that sees itself as "the fixer crew" may habitually overfunction, rescuing failing initiatives but burning out in the process.
- An IT department with the narrative of "always being the bottleneck" might avoid proactive collaboration out of fear of reinforcing that identity.
- A merging organization that sees itself as "losing our legacy" may resist integration efforts, even if the strategy is sound.

These narratives are often unspoken, but they influence risk-taking, innovation, and emotional resilience. They show up in metaphors ("we're firefighting again"), decisions ("we'll stay quiet in this meeting"), and energy levels ("this always happens to us").

Narrative capacity, then, is not just about telling stories but also about recognizing, reshaping, and realigning the stories teams live by. When leaders create space for teams to surface and reauthor those narratives, they tap into a powerful source of identity and change readiness.

Why Narrative Capacity Matters in Projects

In complex and fast-paced environments, projects often feel fragmented. One team is focused on system migration, another on user engagement, a third on change communications. Without a shared narrative, effort becomes transactional. People lose sight of why their work matters. **Narrative capacity brings cohesion.** It aligns purpose with progress. It connects milestones to meaning. It enables teams to make sense of their journey while they are still in it, not only in hindsight.

For Project Leaders: Narrative Capacity as a Core Leadership Tool for Project Delivery

Project leaders sit at the intersection of urgency, complexity, and coordination. They navigate shifting priorities, diverse personalities, and relentless pace, all while staying accountable for outcomes. In this dynamic environment, narrative capacity becomes more than a communication tool, it's a leadership asset that helps teams stay resilient, connected, and purpose-driven. Developing narrative capacity enables project leaders to:

- Build resilience—by helping teams reframe setbacks as part of a meaningful journey.
- Create clarity—by using story structure to interpret ambiguity and chart progress.

- Strengthen engagement—through shared storytelling that fosters trust and belonging.
- Drive strategic alignment—by linking daily execution to a broader purpose and vision.

When project teams can articulate the story they are living—"a turning point," "a building phase," "a comeback moment"—they stay more connected to one another and to their purpose.

For Change Leaders: Reframing Identity and Ownership

Change leaders work across silos to guide people through ambiguity. Narrative becomes their bridge between disruption and integration.

- Sensemaking: Stories help surface how people feel about the change, not just what they think.
- Cocreation: Stories invite participation and shared authorship.
- Reframing: Narratives allow teams to reinterpret fear, loss, or resistance as meaningful transition.

Change leaders who embed leadership narrative playbacks, or metaphor mapping into their practices find that people are more willing to engage with uncertainty when they can place themselves in the unfolding narrative.

For Executive Leaders: Seeing the System Through Story

Executive leaders shape the organizational tone. They make meaning at scale, intentionally or not. Kools and Kearns (2022) highlight the importance of systems-level leadership dialogue, emphasizing that change is sustained not by mandates but by multivoice, reflective conversations that expose dominant narratives and make space for new ones.

Executives benefit from narrative capacity because:

- It surfaces hidden dynamics: Stories reveal cultural patterns, trust gaps, and misaligned expectations.

- It humanizes data: Metrics become meaningful when framed in a journey.
- It shapes culture: Repeated stories signal what the organization values.

When executives listen deeply to frontline narratives, especially those that challenge assumptions, they gain a systems view no dashboard can provide.

As Berger (2019) notes, we are story-driven beings. Teams and organizations that cultivate narrative coherence are more adaptive, emotionally grounded, and committed to the long arc of transformation. Narrative capacity, then, is not just a communication tool but also a strategic, relational, and cultural force that supports leadership at every level.

Narrative capacity brings cohesion. It helps teams connect progress with purpose and setbacks with meaning. It turns scattered activity into a sense of journey, of moving through something together.

Importantly, narrative capacity is not just beneficial at the individual or team level. As Kools and Kearns (2022) argue in their work on systems-level change, effective leadership dialogue must operate across three dimensions: the individual, the relational, and the systemic. At the systemic level, narratives become carriers of cultural assumptions, policy inertia, and power dynamics. Without active narrative reflection, systemic patterns remain invisible and therefore unchangeable.

Kools and Kearns (2022) further suggest that systems can only shift when leaders engage in multivoice, reflective dialogue that surfaces diverse stories and makes space for narrative tension. In this light, building narrative capacity is more than a developmental practice; it's a systems leadership imperative. It helps teams not only interpret their current project but also reshape the very system in which the project unfolds.

Barriers to Narrative in Project Contexts

Despite the value of narrative capacity, several real-world pressures conspire to suppress it. Consider a large-scale enterprise resource planning (ERP) implementation in a global manufacturer. The project team, under strict deadlines, defaulted to rigid stand-ups and progress updates, leaving no room for reflection. As tensions mounted between IT and operations, project leaders noted missed signals, frustrations that could have been surfaced earlier had team members been encouraged to share their stories of confusion or early workarounds.

Despite its value, narrative work can feel unfamiliar or risky in project settings. Time pressures, delivery metrics, and the perception of storytelling as "soft" can make leaders hesitant to explore this domain.

Common barriers include:

- Overemphasis on efficiency: Stories take time and are not easily quantifiable.
- Cultural norms of objectivity: Some environments value data over dialogue.
- Fear of vulnerability: Sharing narrative often means revealing uncertainty or emotion.
- Siloed communication: When teams operate in isolation, shared meaning erodes.

Leaders can consciously create space for narrative reflection, by modeling vulnerability, celebrating sensemaking, and legitimizing story-based learning.

Practices That Build Narrative Capacity

Building narrative capacity doesn't require professional storytellers. It involves creating repeatable practices that invite story, reflection, and identity work.

Here are four examples:

1. Leadership Narrative Playbacks—Small group reflections guided by prompts like:
   "What's a moment of surprise you experienced this sprint?"
   "What would the title of this week's chapter be?"
   This is particularly useful during retrospectives, transitions, or team onboarding.

2. "What Chapter Are We In?" Check-ins

    At key milestones, ask team members to name the chapter they think the project is in. Responses may include "weathering the storm," "turning the page," or "finding our voice." The metaphors surface how people are interpreting change.

3. End-of-Project Storytelling

    In addition to final reports and lessons learned exercises, invite individuals to share brief narratives: What challenged me? What did I learn? What will I take forward? These collective stories can inform leadership insights and team culture.

4. Failure as a Narrative Opportunity

    When things go wrong, invite the team to reconstruct the narrative arc: What happened? What did we expect? What do we now know? This reframes failure as part of a learning journey, not a final verdict.

Dual-Lens Retrospective Canvas

To operationalize the Dual-Lens Framework for narrative reflection, project teams can use a structured tool (Tool 6) during retrospectives. An example version of the canvas is provided in Table 5.1.

Table 5.1 Dual-Lens Retrospective Canvas

Prompt	Lens 1: Experience	Lens 2: Purpose/Function
What stood out to me this sprint?	Emotional highs/lows? Turning points? Surprises?	What conversations moved things forward?
How did I feel in key moments?	Supported? Uncertain? Energized?	What function did the conversation serve (e.g., alignment, transformation)?
What story would I tell about this week?	Title this chapter. What's the narrative arc?	What was I trying to accomplish through my dialogue?
What are we learning about ourselves as a team?	What patterns or themes are emerging?	Are we using conversation strategically? Where are the gaps?
What do we need more/less of in our dialogue?	Space, safety, listening, clarity?	What intentional function should we focus on next?

Teams can complete this individually or in small groups, then synthesize shared themes. Over time, the canvas becomes a learning archive, documenting not just what happened but how the team made sense of it.

Let's look at an example to demonstrate how the **Dual-Lens Retrospective Canvas** works in practice. Below is a realistic, grounded scenario that illustrates its use in a project setting, with clear connections to both Lens 1 (experience) and Lens 2 (function).

Mini-Case: Using the Dual-Lens Retrospective in a Digital Transformation Project

Context:
A midsize Canadian municipality, Fallingbrook County (fictitious name), launched a digital transformation initiative to modernize its public services portal. The project involved multiple departments, IT, citizen services, procurement, and external consultants. After Phase 1 (platform launch), the project manager, Kiran, introduced the **Dual-Lens Retrospective Canvas** during the sprint review.

The Setup:
Each team member completed the canvas individually, followed by small-group discussion and a full-team debrief. They were asked to focus on the past four-week sprint (Table 5.2).

Insights and Outcomes:
The retrospective uncovered a misalignment between project pace and collective understanding. The team was delivering, but many didn't feel connected to why they were doing what they were doing. Kiran realized that while task coordination was strong, the strategic and transformational functions of conversation were being neglected.
Following the debrief:

- Kiran shifted Monday stand-ups to include a rotating narrative prompt: "What part of the story are we in?"

Table 5.2 Highlights from the Canvas exercise

Prompt	Lens 1: Experience	Lens 2: Purpose/Function
What stood out to me this sprint?	"When the public feedback went live, seeing real users struggle was eye-opening."	"The daily stand-up I led helped surface early warnings before they turned into crises."
How did I feel in key moments?	"Tense and reactive, especially when the vendor missed the deadline."	"When I reached out directly to procurement to clear a roadblock, I was trying to realign the project."
What story would I tell about this week?	"This was the cliffhanger chapter, things didn't go as expected, but we improvised."	"We moved from execution mode to adaptive coordination, that shift mattered."
What are we learning about ourselves?	"We tend to silo under stress. We need intentional cross-talk earlier."	"Our conversations are strong in task delivery but weaker in strategic alignment. That's where we lose sight of purpose."
What do we need more/less of?	"More room for reflection; less reacting to emails as emergencies."	"More sensemaking. Fewer rushed status reports. We need to slow down to speed up."

- Change leads began using story fragments (e.g., "chapter titles," "turning points") in communications with stakeholders to humanize progress updates.
- The executive sponsor was invited to the next retrospective, not just to listen to metrics but to hear team stories directly.

The use of the **Dual-Lens Retrospective Canvas** became a turning point in project team culture, from delivery-centric to meaning-aware. This cultural shift didn't happen by chance, it was enabled by an environment where people felt safe to reflect, share, and reframe their experiences together. The Dual-Lens Retrospective Canvas helped unlock a more reflective, meaning-aware culture, but sustaining that shift required more than tools. It required trust. Narrative work depends on psychological safety, where individuals feel secure enough to share unpolished stories, explore uncertainty, and cocreate meaning without fear of judgment.

Psychological Safety and Narrative Work

Narrative capacity thrives in environments of psychological safety. When people feel safe to share unfinished thoughts, vulnerable moments, or dissenting views, storytelling deepens.

Leaders play a pivotal role. They model the behaviors that make narrative work possible, humility, curiosity, and transparency. As Amy Edmondson's (2019) research highlights, teams with high psychological safety learn faster and adapt more effectively, in part because they engage in open sensemaking.

At WynnTech, Elena noticed that the more she shared her own "messy middle," the more others brought their full selves to the table. Over time, narrative practices became not just rituals but sources of renewal.

Mini-Case: Reflective Debriefs in Action—Leadership Perspectives

Findings from our earlier research with senior leaders during major transformation initiatives revealed the five evolving perspectives on leadership conversation, from strategically intentional to catalyzing change, fostering mindful awareness, building shared commitment, and ultimately guiding transformation. These categories mirror the developmental potential of narrative work in teams. As leaders move from managing tasks to co-creating meaning, narrative practices become less about reporting and more about reauthoring the team's identity and direction. Conversations shift from transactional check-ins to intentional spaces of reflection and renewal, supporting the project as both technical initiative and human journey.

At a global infrastructure business known for its high-stakes, technically complex projects, reflective practice was often limited to lessons-learned PowerPoint decks and post-project key performance indicators (KPIs). But one senior project director saw a deeper opportunity. Drawing from her own learning during a leadership development program, she proposed a new approach.

Project Closeout Storytelling

This approach asked each team member to respond to three questions at the conclusion of major initiatives:

1. What was a defining moment for you on this project?
2. What did this project teach you about leadership?
3. What story will you take with you?

The results were powerful, not only because of the insights shared but because of how the practice took root across the organization. What truly transformed the culture was the way project leaders, change leaders, and senior leaders each began to interpret, apply, and amplify the approach through the lens of their distinct roles. Their collective engagement created alignment, momentum, and a shared language for leading change. Let's look at this example.

The Project Leader's View: Cocreating the Story

For Emma, a senior project manager leading a cross-border infrastructure upgrade, the storytelling sessions were a turning point. Her previous debriefs had focused on earned value, risk registers, and milestone charts. While useful, they rarely captured the emotional and relational journey of the team.

During the storytelling narrative playback, one engineer shared how a late-night decision Emma made to shift timelines saved not just the schedule but the team's morale. "I felt like we were finally trusted," he said. Emma hadn't realized how pivotal that moment had been.

She later reflected: "The numbers told one story. But their stories showed me what leadership looked like in practice."

For Emma, narrative became both mirror and map, reflecting back her impact and guiding how she would lead future teams. She began using micro-storytelling check-ins during sprint reviews, asking team members to share "one sentence from this week's chapter." The effect was subtle, but over time, it changed how the team engaged, less guarded, more generative.

The Change Leader's View: Reframing Identity

Greg, the organization's senior change leader, recognized the potential for storytelling to shift how people internalized transformation. He noticed a pattern in the debriefs: Teams that had faced the most tension were often the ones whose stories revealed the greatest learning and growth.
He began using aggregated narratives to facilitate transition workshops:

- "Here's what we've heard from your colleagues across five projects …"
- "What themes resonate with your experience?"

Through this approach, Greg moved beyond presenting top-down change roadmaps to curating stories that allowed teams to see themselves in the arc of transformation. He adapted the closeout questions to midstream change assessments, enabling narrative "rechecks" at key moments.

"Story isn't just reflection, it's reframing. These narratives helped teams move from disruption to identity. They started to see the change not as something happening to them, but something they were shaping."

The Executive Leader's View: Learning the System

At the executive level, Aisha, the firm's VP of Delivery, initially saw storytelling as "soft" data. But after reading several team storybooks compiled from debriefs, she noticed something consistent: misalignments between stated values and lived experience. Teams often cited breakdowns in decision making, ambiguity around ownership, or moments when informal leadership had stepped up in the absence of formal clarity.

Rather than react defensively, Aisha leaned in. She began commissioning story-based summaries alongside traditional project close reports, and invited storytelling reps to executive debriefs.

One insight that stood out: "Trust gaps don't start in delivery. They start in how projects are launched."

That statement prompted a shift in how early-stage planning was structured. From then on, prelaunch meetings included a "narrative intention" round, asking leaders: "What story do we hope this project tells in the end, and what might get in the way?"

Aisha later commented: "The stories gave me a systems view that no dashboard ever could. They revealed what people navigate in the white space between our charts."

This mini-case vividly reflects our research insights, leaders moving from strategically intentional to transformational conversations. Each of the three leaders embodies a distinct way of integrating narrative:

- Emma (Project Leader) focuses on awareness and team identity.
- Greg (Change Leader) uses story to reframe roles and increase ownership.
- Aisha (Executive Leader) sees stories as systemic signals and acts on them to align strategy and culture.

Together, they show how reflective storytelling isn't a one-time intervention but rather a multilevel leadership practice that connects experience with transformation. The shift was subtle but profound. Patterns emerged across projects, on trust, timelines, and client alignment. These insights shaped training, resource planning, and even executive messaging. By surfacing stories instead of just metrics, the business built a feedback culture rooted in reflection.

This mini-case illustrates how reflective debriefs create space for shared insight, leadership growth, and alignment across roles. To help you apply these practices in your own context, leaders can locate the Reflective Storytelling Worksheet (Tool 7) in Appendix D. It offers a guided structure for turning meaningful dialogue into actionable leadership insight.

Integrating the Dual-Lens Framework

Narrative capacity sits at the intersection of experience and intention. Lens 1 reveals how people experience conversation, whether they feel heard, shaped, stretched. Lens 2 examines what those conversations are trying to do, align, transform, clarify.

When leaders attend to both lenses, they begin to ask different questions:

- Am I inviting stories, or just updates?
- Are we treating this conversation as a tool, or as a space for identity work?
- What function does this narrative serve in the change we're leading?

Narrative capacity doesn't just reflect a strong team, it develops one. It grows shared understanding and shapes the tone and trajectory of transformation.

Reflective Prompts

- When was the last time you invited your team to tell a story, about success, failure, or transition?
- What narrative is shaping how your team sees this change?
- What chapter are you in as a leader right now?
- How can narrative capacity support alignment across silos or stakeholder groups?

Learning Outcomes

The following outcomes summarize the knowledge and skills you've developed in this chapter:

- Explain the neuroscience of storytelling and its impact on connection, empathy, and memory.
- Identify and craft different types of leadership stories (origin, failure, customer, team, future) for strategic impact.
- Apply the Dual-Lens Storytelling Checklist to ensure stories are both authentic (Lens 1) and purposive (Lens 2).
- Facilitate team storytelling practices that strengthen narrative capacity and cultural alignment.

A Glimpse Ahead

Storytelling gives shape to experience, helping teams understand where they've been, who they are, and what matters most. But as change accelerates and interdependencies grow, even the best-crafted stories can begin to feel incomplete. In complex environments, there is no single narrative that explains it all. Meaning becomes fluid, and leadership requires a new kind of presence.

In Chapter 6, we move from narrative clarity to navigating ambiguity. We explore what it means to lead through complexity, where there are no clear answers, only patterns, tensions, and emerging possibilities. You'll discover how strategic sensemaking, systems thinking, and conversational awareness helps leaders stay grounded and effective amid uncertainty. By learning to read the signals beneath the noise, leaders can cultivate the insight and responsiveness needed to guide transformation, even when the path ahead is still unfolding.

"Leadership Reflection Break"

"Although you can't reach everyone, you have reached enough that between what you have been able to achieve and what they are hearing is consistent. As a leader you are trying to build that common vision across everyone in the organization, which is the ultimate goal, working through my peers and direct reports is one of the tactics to getting there. Getting them to become leaders, getting those managers inspired and to become leaders, keeping the eye on the ultimate goal and reaching all employees in the end is key."

CHAPTER 6

Storytelling for Alignment and Action

Opening Scene: The Story Behind the Slide Deck

The numbers made sense, but the expressions around the table told a more complex story, one about readiness, resistance, and unspoken concerns.

Elena adjusted her blazer as she stepped into the glass-walled boardroom, sunlight cutting sharp angles across the polished conference table. The senior leadership team had gathered, each carrying a different thread of anxiety about the upcoming transformation phase. Elena had fifteen minutes to deliver more than a project update; she had to align the room. She began not with metrics, but with a story. "Let me tell you about Marcus," she said, referring to one of the regional project managers. "Last month, when the rollout faced sudden pushback in the Northern region, Marcus did something we all can learn from."

As the room quieted, Elena narrated how Marcus gathered his cross-functional team for a two-hour dialogue. He started not with a briefing but with a shared story-building exercise: "If this transformation were a journey, where are we now, and where do we fear it might go?" The responses, "a detour we didn't choose," "a foggy pass," and "nearing a breakthrough" shifted the conversation. The team moved from technical updates to emotional truth. Elena's retelling of Marcus's moment set the tone. For the next fifteen minutes, the executive team listened, truly listened. It wasn't just about the facts. It was about meaning.

This chapter explores how leaders use storytelling to align people around strategy, purpose, and coordinated action, particularly in times of uncertainty, resistance, or transition. It examines how narrative can bridge the gap between vision and execution, positioning storytelling as a powerful leadership lever for alignment and strategic transformation. Through story, leaders can connect individuals, teams, and systems to a shared direction and mobilize them toward meaningful, collective action.

"If people can't see themselves in the story, they won't follow where it's going."

At every level of a project or change effort, alignment is critical, but hard to achieve. Despite clear plans and cascading emails, people often interpret messages through their own filters: job function, role, history, or level of trust in leadership. That's where storytelling becomes a strategic asset.

Story as a Tool for Strategic Alignment

Strategic plans often fail not because of faulty logic but because of emotional disconnect. Storytelling helps leaders bridge the gap between intention and engagement. It translates abstract goals into shared language and lived experience. In projects, especially those involving change, stories provide a throughline, an emotional and cognitive map of where we are, where we've been, and where we're going.

During a recent consulting engagement, I encountered a situation that illustrates this well.

Mini-Case: "The Mirror Room"—The Context

Bishop Tech (fictitious name), a midsize software development company, had recently undergone a major rebranding effort. The executive team was excited: new colors, new messaging, a renewed promise to customers about innovation and agility. But two months in, momentum stalled. Sales teams kept pitching the old value propositions. Marketing wasn't aligned on the messaging. Developers felt like the changes were cosmetic. Morale dipped. A consulting team was brought in to diagnose the breakdown in alignment.

The Discovery

Through one-on-one interviews and group workshops, the consultants unearthed a pattern: There was no shared understanding of why the rebrand mattered. Leadership had assumed that the rationale behind the change, staying competitive in a shifting tech landscape, was obvious. But employees felt blindsided, confused, and disconnected from the strategy.

One manager described it as "decorating the living room while the foundation is cracking."

The Leadership Conversation

The consultants organized a facilitated session called "The Mirror Room" where leaders were asked to reflect on how their communication had contributed to the disconnection. The VP of Sales admitted he hadn't fully bought into the new message either:

"I kept telling my team to 'just go with it' because I didn't want to slow things down. But now I realize, we weren't moving at all."

The CTO added, "We told ourselves this was a signal to the market. But we didn't think about the signal it sent to our own people."

These admissions weren't just symbolic; they were catalytic.

Creating Shared Meaning

In a follow-up workshop, the consultants introduced a storytelling exercise: Each leader had to write a personal narrative answering the question "Why does this change matter to me, and how will I help others see it?" These were then shared across teams. One story, by the head of product, sparked real traction; he linked the change to a moment early in his career when customer feedback saved his team from a failed launch. "We're evolving not because it looks good, but because our survival depends on listening."

This grounded the change in something real. Authentic. Relatable.

The Shift

By the next month:

- Leaders hosted "meaningful conversations" in small groups instead of town halls.
- Messaging decks were rewritten collaboratively across departments.
- Employees began contributing their own change narratives in internal forums.

A new culture was established, not just of change but of ownership and leadership connection through conversation.

A dynamic, people-centered session framework (see Appendix E: Framing Our Collective Story) is designed to help leaders foster connection, cocreate meaning, and build momentum, particularly valuable during periods of change, transition, or team realignment.

Why Storytelling Works

Sessions like this do more than generate good conversation; they activate something deeper. Storytelling changes how people feel, process, and remember. Research in neuroscience shows that stories are uniquely powerful because they engage both the emotional and logical centers of the brain. When people hear a well-told story, their brains don't just listen but also simulate. Oxytocin is released, trust is enhanced, and understanding deepens.

This is why stories are so essential in leadership dialogue:

- They build emotional connection. Facts inform, but stories stick.
- They create shared meaning. Stories help us understand not just what's changing but why it matters.
- They reveal values and beliefs. Personal narratives demonstrate authenticity, humility, and purpose.

When leaders use storytelling to align and inspire action, they combine empathy, attentive listening, and vulnerability with adaptability and

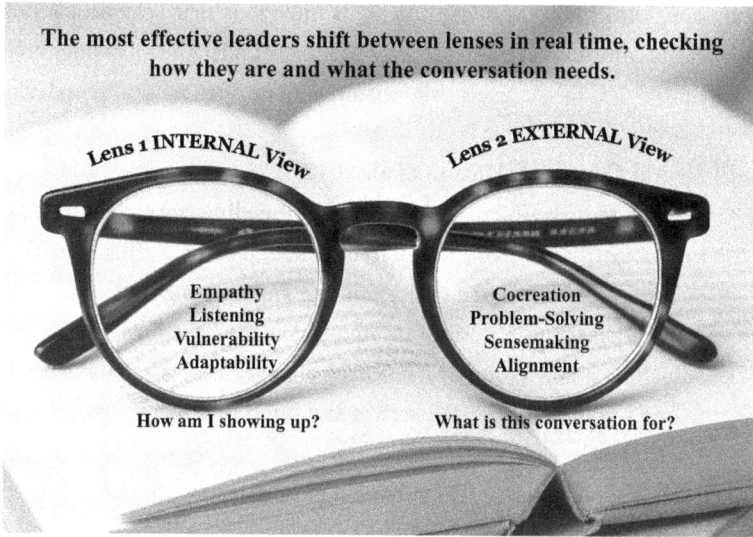

Figure 6.1 Understanding the lenses

cocreation. Through problem-solving, sensemaking, and alignment, these stories become more than messages; they become shared narratives that move people toward a common vision and tangible next steps.

Understanding the lenses (Figure 6.1) is a reminder that the most impactful leaders continually check both their internal stance and the external intention of the conversation, adjusting in real time.

The Neuroscience of Storytelling in Leadership

Research shows that storytelling engages more of the brain than data alone. When someone hears a compelling story, their brain activity begins to mirror the storyteller's, a phenomenon known as neural coupling. This phenomenon is observed in various social interactions, especially during verbal communication, and storytelling. Paul Zak (2018) found that emotionally resonant narratives trigger the release of oxytocin, increasing empathy and connection. Story structure activates sensory, emotional, and motor systems, making information more memorable and decisions more aligned with values.

This means storytelling is not simply a communication tool but also a biological experience. And because stories activate sensory, emotional, and motor regions, they create vivid mental simulations that help people not only retain information but feel motivated to act on it. The following three key neurological mechanisms help explain why storytelling is so powerful.

1. **Neural Coupling (Hasson et al. 2012)**

   What it means: When a leader tells a compelling story, the listener's brain begins to mirror the storyteller's neural activity. This "neural coupling" creates shared understanding and alignment.

   Leadership Application: In high-stakes conversations, like launching a new vision or navigating change, leaders can use storytelling to synchronize perspectives and build trust.

   Example:

   During a town hall, a CEO shares a personal story about her first failed start-up and how it taught her resilience. As she speaks, employees begin to feel her vulnerability and determination. Instead of just hearing "we need to be agile," they feel it. Her story aligns their mindset with hers, making the message stick far more than a slide deck ever could.

2. **Oxytocin and Empathy (Zak 2018)**

   What it means: Emotionally resonant stories release oxytocin, a neurochemical that increases empathy and connection. This makes listeners more likely to trust, cooperate, and act.

   Leadership Application: When leaders want to inspire action, especially in moments of tension or resistance, stories that evoke emotion can shift behavior more effectively than logic alone.

   Example:

   A manager addressing burnout in her team doesn't just cite statistics. She shares a story about a colleague who missed his daughter's recital due to work stress, and how it led to a teamwide rethink of priorities. The story triggers empathy, and the team becomes more open to adopting new wellness practices, not because they were told to but because they care.

3. **Sensory, Emotional, and Motor Activation (Zak 2018)**

   What it means: Story structure activates multiple brain systems, sensory (imagery), emotional (feelings), and motor (action), making the message more memorable and values-driven.

Leadership Application: In strategic planning or culture-building conversations, leaders can use vivid, value-based stories to anchor decisions in shared meaning.

Example:

A nonprofit director tells the story of a refugee family they helped resettle. She describes the smell of the airport, the child's wide eyes, and the first warm meal. The team doesn't just remember the mission; they embody it. Later, when debating budget cuts, they prioritize programs that align with that story's emotional core.

Why This Matters for Change

Storytelling isn't just decoration but also a neurological tool for transformation. Leaders who intentionally use story:

- Create alignment through shared brain activity.
- Build trust through emotional resonance.
- Anchor values through multisensory engagement.

The following examples offer meaningful insight into how this plays out in practice.

Storytelling in Project Implementation: A Leadership Advantage

1. **Neural Coupling—Building Shared Vision**
   Example:
   When launching a new customer relationship management (CRM) system, the project lead kicks off the initiative not with a technical briefing, but by telling the story of "Jenny," a long-time sales rep who once lost a major deal because she didn't have the right client data in time. The leader paints a picture of frustration, missed opportunity, and the human cost of inefficient systems.

   As the team listens, their brains begin to mirror the story, understanding not just what needs to be done but why it matters. Neural coupling helps employees feel aligned from the start, reducing resistance and increasing ownership.

2. **Oxytocin Release—Building Trust and Empathy**
   Example:
   Midway through the project, things get tough. Deadlines slip. Tensions rise. Instead of issuing warnings or lectures, the PM shares a story about a previous rollout that nearly failed, but ultimately succeeded thanks to team resilience and mutual support.

   He describes the emotional toll, but also the triumph. The story creates a release of oxytocin, prompting empathy across the team. People shift from blame to collaboration. A developer volunteers to work late, not because she's told to but because she cares about the outcome.

3. **Multisystem Activation—Making the Plan Stick**
   Example:
   When presenting the final phase of implementation to senior stakeholders, the sponsor uses narrative rather than data alone. He describes walking into the call center, seeing agents navigate the new dashboard for the first time. He adds sensory detail, the flickering monitors, the hum of phones, the agent who finally says, "This makes sense!"

   By engaging sensory (imagery), emotional (frustration and relief), and motor (action and change) systems, the message doesn't just inform, it sticks. Stakeholders remember the impact more than the milestones.

Bottom Line: Leaders Who Tell Stories Move Projects Forward

Storytelling transforms dry updates into energizing conversations. It helps teams:

- Grasp complexity by anchoring it in human experience.
- Navigate setbacks with compassion and creativity.
- Align around purpose, not just process.

Cascading Narrative: Layers of Alignment

Alignment doesn't happen through a single message. It requires cascading stories that are adapted at each layer of the organization. A CEO might share a vision of "becoming the most trusted energy partner in the region." A VP reframes it as "ensuring every client interaction builds confidence." A frontline supervisor translates it into: "Every customer call is a moment of trust."

These aren't different stories; they're the same story retold at different levels. Leaders must ensure that each version maintains narrative integrity while speaking to its audience's context.

Audience Alignment: Tailoring the Story

Effective stories do not just resonate but also reflect. Leaders need to consider: Who is the audience? What do they care about? What emotions or narratives are already in play? What's the desired shift, in thinking, feeling, or action?

For example, project teams might respond to metaphors about momentum and achievement, while HR teams may connect with stories of belonging and legacy. Storytelling becomes a tool not just for alignment but for inclusion.

Overcoming Resistance Through Coauthored Narrative

Resistance often emerges from unacknowledged or outdated narratives: "We tried this before," "This will only benefit HQ," "It's not our story."

Leaders can address resistance not by countering these stories, but by inviting their authorship.

In one financial institution, a change leader ran "legacy story" sessions, where employees told the story of past transformations. Facilitators helped the team identify themes, resilience, fear, innovation, and then invited them to cocreate the new narrative: "This time, what's different?"

The Dual-Lens Framework in Practice

To use storytelling effectively as a leadership tool, it's not enough to simply tell engaging stories. Leaders must reflect on both how the story will be experienced and what the story is intended to accomplish. This is where the Dual-Lens Framework becomes an invaluable guide.

The framework introduces two distinct but complementary perspectives:

- **Lens 1: Experience**—How are stories interpreted by different people?
- **Lens 2: Function**—What is the story meant to do?

Together, these lenses help leaders move from simply sharing information to using storytelling as a strategic intervention, one that shapes meaning, builds trust, supports understanding, and enables transformation.

Let's break this down further.

Understanding Lens 1: Experience

Lens 1 prompts leaders to consider how a story is received. It recognizes that no two people hear the same message in the same way. Personal experiences, organizational history, power dynamics, identity, and emotional readiness all influence how stories land.

A story about "bold risk-taking," for example, might energize executives, while making frontline teams, already under pressure, feel unsafe or excluded.

Leaders must cultivate the awareness to ask:

- How might others interpret this story?
- What histories or emotions could be triggered or affirmed?
- Whose experience is being centered, and whose is being left out?

This internal sensitivity equips leaders to tell stories that are not just engaging but inclusive and attuned to the emotional landscape of their teams.

Understanding Lens 2: Function

While Lens 1 focuses on how a story is heard, **Lens 2** focuses on what the story is for. Every leadership conversation, and every story within it, has an implicit or explicit function. The Dual-Lens model identifies five primary functions of leadership storytelling (Table 6.1):

Table 6.1 Lens 2 storytelling

Function	Purpose
Transmission	Delivering direction, communicating a message clearly
Relationship	Building trust, sharing values, showing vulnerability
Sensemaking	Helping teams interpret change or uncertainty
Alignment	Connecting individual actions to a broader purpose
Transformation	Reframing identity or inviting mindset shifts

A single story may serve more than one function. What matters is that the leader knows what they're trying to achieve through the story, and chooses their framing accordingly.

For instance, a story about early pushback in a project can serve multiple functions:

- **Sensemaking**, by naming shared confusion
- **Relationship**, by showing humility
- **Alignment**, by reconnecting efforts to purpose

Why Intentional Storytelling Matters

Intentional storytelling is especially powerful during moments of ambiguity, transition, or resistance. It transforms a story from anecdote into intervention. For example:

- A story meant to inform may land flat if the audience craves inspiration.
- A story that aims to motivate may backfire if people don't feel heard.
- A story that seeks to clarify may instead confuse, if it doesn't account for what people already believe.

This is why the Dual-Lens Framework is essential. It gives leaders a way to pause and ask:

- What meaning might others take from this?
- What am I trying to accomplish?
- Is this the right story, and is it being told in the right way?

Table 6.2 Integrating the Dual Lenses—Lens 2 storytelling

Conversation function	Storytelling purpose	Example
Transmission	Deliver a core message	Share a past failure that reinforces the need for new processes
Relationship	Build connection and trust	Share a personal mistake that led to learning
Sensemaking	Interpret change together	Use metaphor or analogy to explain ambiguity
Alignment	Reinforce shared purpose	Link daily work to mission through story
Transformation	Shift identity or perspective	Reauthor team or org narrative after a setback

Integrating the Dual Lenses

Table 6.2 connects **Lens 2 functions** with their practical storytelling applications.

Using both lenses, what people hear and what you hope to achieve, enables leaders to lead through story, not just communicate through it.

Dual-Lens Storytelling Checklist

To support this reflective practice, the following Dual-Lens Storytelling Checklist can be used to plan, reflect on, or evaluate leadership storytelling moments. The checklist is structured around the five categories of experience (Lens 1) and the five functions of storytelling (Lens 2).

This design allows leaders to check both the interpretive readiness of their audience and their own strategic purpose. It can be used before a high-stakes presentation, in a change rollout, or as part of a regular leadership reflection routine.

Lens 1: Experience

How might others experience this story, emotionally, cognitively, or relationally?

- Strategic Intent—Am I aware of the power dynamics or assumptions I may be reinforcing through this story?

Could this narrative unintentionally signal compliance or control rather than collaboration?

- Shared Commitment—Have I considered how different roles (e.g., frontline, project team, senior execs) might hear this story?
  Does the story resonate across perspectives and build inclusion?
- Mindful Awareness—Am I aware of any cultural, historical, or organizational narratives that could shape interpretation?
  Is the story sensitive to underlying beliefs, identities, or trauma?
- Guiding the Change—Have I invited feedback or listened to how the story landed?
  Does the story prompt conversation or reflection beyond its telling?
- Catalyst for Change—Does the story make space for others to bring their own experiences?
  Is the narrative open-ended enough to spark imagination, reframe thinking, or invite cocreation?

Lens 2: Function

What am I trying to accomplish with this story?

- Transmission—Am I clearly communicating a direction, decision, or priority? Is the story helping simplify a complex message?
- Relationship—Am I building trust through vulnerability or shared experience? Does the story reflect my values or show empathy?
- Sensemaking—Am I helping others understand uncertainty or change? Have I used metaphor or narrative framing to support comprehension?
- Alignment—Does the story connect individual or team contributions to a larger purpose? Have I framed the "why" behind what we're doing?
- Transformation—Am I helping others see themselves, or our organization, in a new light? Could this story invite a shift in mindset, identity, or culture?

Before You Share:
Have I rehearsed or reflected on how this story might sound to someone unlike me? Have I asked, "Why this story, now?"

After You Share:
What feedback did I notice, verbal, nonverbal, emotional? Did the story achieve its intended function? Is there a follow-up conversation or narrative I now need to support?

Let's look at a Mini-Case from WynnTech

Elena, Marcus, and Nia each found distinct ways to use storytelling not as an embellishment but as a core leadership practice to drive alignment and engagement.

Elena began intentionally incorporating story arcs into her leadership updates. Rather than presenting status metrics in isolation, she contextualized progress within a broader narrative, highlighting purpose, tension, and resolution. After hearing one of Marcus's field updates framed as a learning moment, she shared it with the senior leadership team as an example of frontline insight informing strategic clarity. In doing so, she repositioned Marcus's voice as a bridge between execution and strategy. Over time, she encouraged all project leads to submit short narrative snapshots for leadership briefings, creating a rhythm of story-informed dialogue across levels.

Marcus introduced metaphor mapping in his change management sessions. He asked teams to express where they were emotionally in the change process using image-based metaphors: "We're in the fog," "We're climbing a steep hill," "We're on a bridge, but the other side isn't clear yet." These metaphors made it safe to voice uncertainty, surface unspoken fears, and visualize momentum. He posted the metaphors on a project wall, and during each check-in, teams reflected on whether their image still resonated, or needed to evolve. One team moved from "adrift at sea" to "setting our sails"—a subtle yet powerful shift in ownership and agency.

Nia, reflecting on the early resistance her team showed toward project milestones and shifting requirements, reframed her weekly stand-ups with "chapter check-ins." Rather than reviewing deliverables line by line, she would begin with: "What part of the story are we in this week?" The question became a conversational prompt. Team members began using storytelling language: "This week feels like rising action," "We're nearing a turning point," or "That setback was our plot twist." These shared metaphors helped normalize turbulence and built narrative resilience, reminding the team that challenges were not failure, but expected elements of a larger journey.

Across all three leaders, stories moved from message to meaning, from reporting to reflection, and from compliance to coauthorship. Each found ways to use storytelling not just to align tasks but to reinforce purpose, reframe resistance, and reconnect people to the human dimensions of change.

Why Alignment Fails Without Narrative

Without story, strategy remains abstract. Change feels imposed. People disengage. Common failures include:

- Mixed messages from different leaders
- Lack of emotional resonance
- Ignoring legacy narratives or cultural subtext

Story acts as connective tissue, aligning action with meaning. It helps people see themselves as protagonists in the change, not passive recipients.

Reflective Prompts

What story is currently shaping our team's identity?

Where is alignment breaking down, and what story could restore it?

How do I use stories to reinforce strategic clarity or emotional connection?

Which narrative functions (transmission, relationship, sensemaking, alignment, transformation) am I most comfortable using? Which are underused?

Learning Outcomes

The following outcomes summarize the knowledge and skills you've developed in this chapter:

- Define narrative capacity and its role in sustaining change momentum.

- Embed narrative practices such as story discussions, legacy interviews, reflection rounds, and culture sprints into team routines.
- Use the Conversation Practice Map and Narrative Inquiry Reflection Worksheet to link storytelling with reflective practice.
- Recognize how narrative capacity at the team level connects to broader organizational identity and culture.

A Glimpse Ahead

Chapter 7 explores how transformation doesn't end with implementation. It is sustained through the rhythms of reflection, conversation, and collective meaning-making. In fast-paced environments, lasting change depends not just on what leaders do but on how they create space to listen, adapt, and renew. This next final chapter shows how project, change, and executive leaders embed reflective practices, like pause, dialogue, and story-sharing, into their daily routines to foster alignment, resilience, and momentum over time.

Drawing on the Dual-Lens Framework, we revisit the heart of narrative leadership: understanding how stories are experienced (Lens 1) and using them with clarity and intention (Lens 2). Chapter 7 invites leaders to cultivate narrative capacity—not just as a skill but as a sustained, strategic way of being.

"Leadership Reflection Break"

"I often look for common ground, sometimes it's a different approach and tactic. When I look at my peers or superiors, there is more done outside of meetings than in the meetings. When you start to look at parts of the business, once we articulate where we are going, how do we engage people first, it's not best done in committees, it's done outside the committee or meeting. There is a need to build a relationship first, establish some context, get understanding first, help them understand and then in meetings its final agreement, it just reinforces what has already been agreed to and understood."

CHAPTER 7

Becoming a Narrative Leader

Opening Scene: The Conversation After the Conversation

Once the official meeting ended, the real dialogue emerged, where meaning was made, alignment tested, and possibilities opened.

The final meeting had no agenda. No slides. No facilitator. Just coffee and a whiteboard scrawled with the words: "What's the story we'll carry forward?"

Elena sat beside Marcus and Nia in the now-familiar project war room; this time the meeting transformed into a storytelling space. Around them, Post-it notes from past retrospectives still clung to the walls. They had gathered their teams through the messiness of transformation, ambiguous priorities, stalled momentum, reluctant stakeholders. But today, it was just the three of them.

Nia broke the silence. "Remember when we thought 'alignment' meant just getting everyone to agree?"

They laughed.

Marcus added, "Turns out alignment is less about agreement, and more about shared interpretation. The stories people tell themselves … That's what shapes momentum."

Elena nodded. "We've each changed too. Not just as leaders, but as people."

This wasn't a project closeout. It was a turning point. Each of them had led differently. Talked differently. Listened differently. And somewhere along the way, they had become something more: narrative leaders.

This final chapter invites leaders to embrace the Dual-Lens Framework not as a static model but as a lifelong reflective practice. Narrative identity is presented as a dynamic, evolving process, one that draws on all five categories of experience and functions of conversation. The chapter supports leaders in weaving storytelling, reflective dialogue, and identity formation into their ongoing leadership journey. At its core, it explores the inner work of leadership, how meaning is made, renewed, and shared over time. The framework becomes not only a tool for planning conversations but also a guide for self-coaching and personal growth. Narrative leaders don't simply tell stories; they engage in intentional conversations that adapt, deepen, and resonate across every dimension of change.

"As a narrative leader, the most powerful story you'll ever tell is the one you live every day."

What It Means to Be a Narrative Leader

In fast-changing, complex environments, leadership is not simply about directing outcomes but also about making meaning. Narrative leadership is the practice of engaging others through conversation, reflection, and story to cocreate understanding, build trust, and foster commitment.

To be a narrative leader is not to master the art of telling great stories. It is to develop the inner and outer voice of leadership: to become someone who listens between the lines, who reframes stuck conversations, and who cultivates spaces where others can find their own voice.

As Stephen Denning (2020) writes, "The most powerful leaders operate through narrative, not because they are performers, but because they understand that story is how people learn, commit, and change."

Narrative leaders use story not only to communicate but to align, to liberate, and to transform.

The Reflective Voice of the Leader

Narrative leadership begins with the leader's own story. Before we can shape organizational narrative, we must first examine our own internal script.

This inner narrative, formed through experience, identity, values, and belief, guides how we show up in conversation. Are we reactive or responsive? Directive or curious? Open or guarded?

Marcus described a moment when he realized his internal narrative was "I have to know everything to be credible." That story drove defensiveness in meetings. Through coaching and reflection, he revised that script: "Credibility comes from curiosity and clarity." The shift changed how he spoke with his team, and how they responded. Narrative self-awareness isn't a luxury; it's a leadership imperative.

"Leadership practice deepens when action is paired with reflection, when meaning-making becomes as intentional as decision making."

Practicing Narrative Inquiry

Narrative inquiry is a tool for surfacing meaning, both individually and in teams. It involves asking reflective, story-based questions that illuminate patterns, choices, and possibilities.

Instead of asking: "What happened?"

Try asking: "What story are you telling yourself about what happened?" "Where does this story come from?" "What alternative story could be just as true?"

Leaders can use narrative inquiry to:

- Reflect on difficult decisions.
- Make sense of conflict or resistance.
- Debrief team dynamics.
- Revisit personal growth moments.

Nia began using narrative inquiry after critical milestones. At her team's retrospectives, she added new questions:

- "What was a moment that changed how you saw this work?"
- "What did this experience reveal about your leadership?"
- "If this project were a chapter in your professional story, what would it be called?"

These questions didn't just generate feedback. They generated perspective.

Leadership Identity as Evolving Story

Leaders often inherit roles that come with implicit scripts: Be decisive. Be tough. Be perfect. But the best leaders rewrite those scripts. As people move into new responsibilities, managing a crisis, scaling a team, or becoming executive sponsors, they must reauthor their leadership identity.

Elena shared how her role shifted from facilitator to steward. "In the beginning, I thought my job was to get people to agree. Later, I realized my job was to help people listen to each other differently."

This reframing reflects an important truth: Leadership isn't fixed. It's iterative. Every change effort is an invitation to revise who we are, and who we are becoming.

Sustaining Narrative Practice in Organizational Life

To lead through strategic change is not only to lead differently but also to build an organization where conversations matter.
Narrative practices can become embedded through:

- Story Discussions: Teams gather to reflect on high and low points of the project.
- Legacy Interviews: Departing employees share stories of key contributions.
- Reflection Rounds: Leaders share how their understanding has evolved.
- Culture Sprints: Teams cocreate the next chapter of their work story.

At WynnTech, Marcus began including a "narrative moment" at monthly team meetings. Each member shared one story that reflected a project value in action. These moments weren't long, but they built cohesion and ownership.

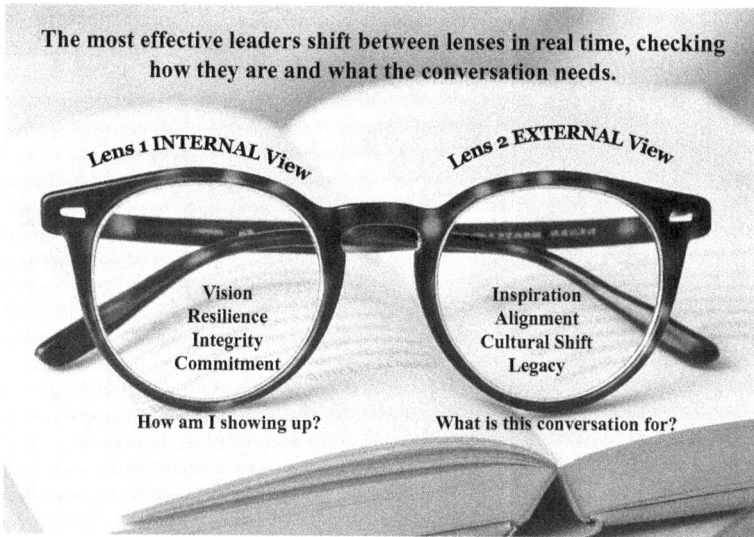

The most effective leaders shift between lenses in real time, checking how they are and what the conversation needs.

Lens 1 INTERNAL View

Lens 2 EXTERNAL View

Vision
Resilience
Integrity
Commitment

Inspiration
Alignment
Cultural Shift
Legacy

How am I showing up?

What is this conversation for?

Figure 7.1 Sustaining a culture of conversational leadership

Nia launched a peer storytelling series, where project leads shared "lessons I didn't expect to learn." It created vulnerability, humor, and learning across silos. Her narrative practice wasn't a communication strategy. It was a cultural rhythm.

Elena began integrating narrative prompts into stakeholder debriefs, asking questions like "What surprised you most during this rollout?" and "What story do you think we'll tell about this project in six months?" These seemingly simple reflections helped surface misalignments early and built a shared sense of learning across departments.

Sustaining a culture of conversational leadership (Figure 7.1) means living in both lenses, staying aware of how you show up while staying intentional about why the conversation matters.

The Dual-Lens Framework Revisited

Throughout this book, we've returned to two essential lenses:

- Lens 1: Experience—How are conversations interpreted?
- Lens 2: Function—What are conversations for?

Narrative leaders operate through both. They recognize that meaning is never one-size-fits-all, conversations are filtered through lived experiences, roles, and emotions. And because of that, they choose their words, tone, and timing with purpose: to inform, connect, clarify, align, or transform.

To help leaders stay anchored in this dual perspective, the **Conversation Practice Map** brings it all together. It offers a practical way to reflect on real conversations, linking **intentional action (Lens 2)** with **interpretive awareness (Lens 1)**. Whether planning a team dialogue, debriefing a stakeholder exchange, or preparing for a moment of uncertainty, this map helps leaders pause, reflect, and choose their conversational posture wisely.

Use the Practice Map as a guide, not just for looking back but for shaping the conversations ahead.

Tool 8: Conversation Practice Map

For each major conversation, ask the questions listed in Table 7.1.

Use this map to audit meetings, messages, or project milestones. Over time, you'll notice your leadership conversations becoming more deliberate and more powerful.

While the Practice Map helps leaders position their conversations within the Dual-Lens Framework, the **Narrative Inquiry Reflection Worksheet** invites a deeper dive, exploring the stories beneath those conversations and the identities they shape, shift, or sustain.

Table 7.1 Conversation Practice Map

Function	Am I using this?	Could I strengthen it?	Notes/ Reflection
Transmission	☐ Yes ☐ No	☐ Yes ☐ No	
Relationship	☐ Yes ☐ No	☐ Yes ☐ No	
Sensemaking	☐ Yes ☐ No	☐ Yes ☐ No	
Alignment	☐ Yes ☐ No	☐ Yes ☐ No	
Transformation	☐ Yes ☐ No	☐ Yes ☐ No	

Tool 9: Narrative Inquiry Reflection Worksheet

Use this with yourself or your team:

1. What was a defining moment in the last project?
2. What did this moment reveal about you as a leader?
3. What story were you telling yourself at that time?
4. How has that story changed?
5. What narrative would you like to cultivate in your next initiative?

By making space for introspection, emotional insight, and meaning-making, the **Narrative Inquiry Reflection Worksheet** helps leaders not just interpret events but evolve through them, deepening their narrative capacity and expanding their impact across teams and transformations. Grounded in the Dual-Lens Framework, the worksheet helps leaders connect how they experience their conversations with what those conversations are designed to achieve, turning personal insight into purposeful action.

Final Reflective Prompt: Your Leadership Legacy

Leadership is not remembered by the plans you wrote, but by the conversations you hosted, the space you held, and the stories you helped shape.

> *"We become the stories we tell ourselves, and the stories we help others tell."*

So ask yourself:

- What story do I want my team to carry forward?
- What leadership story do I want to be remembered for?

Learning Outcomes

The following outcomes summarize the knowledge and skills you've developed in this chapter:

- Integrate the Dual-Lens Framework across executive, change, and project leadership roles.

- Design change strategies that balance internal meaning-making with external alignment and transformation.
- Evaluate leadership conversations as high-leverage interventions in complex systems.
- Commit to ongoing reflective practice using the tools, frameworks, and narrative approaches introduced throughout the book.

A Glimpse Ahead

This book may end, but your leadership story doesn't. Let the conversations you've started continue. Use them to bridge across functions, spark ideas, hold tension, and reframe resistance. To support continued learning and dialogue, I'll leave you with the following Leader/Facilitator Notes that provide a chapter-by-chapter guide for applying the core concepts in real-world settings. Whether you're leading a team, facilitating a workshop, or reflecting on your own growth, these prompts and tools offer a practical bridge from insight to action. You could be leading a project, guiding change, or stewarding strategy, remember:

Change happens one conversation at a time.

Leadership is not just a role but also a narrative. It unfolds in what we say, how we act, what we reflect, and how we respond to the unexpected. By now, you've seen how story can guide teams, align organizations, and shape change. This final chapter has shifted the focus inward: What story are you telling as a leader? And how might you write your next chapter with more intention, clarity, and purpose?

"Leadership Reflection Break"

"The challenges and changes that are to come are more complex than before and they will be extremely challenging for us. We are going to have to find ways to work better collaboratively, as opposed to silos, in order to be successful. This will be so important, the dialogue and discussion, the debate, engaging staff and creating an environment where people feel a part of the solution."

Leader/Facilitator Notes Chapter by Chapter

These notes are designed to support our many leaders, facilitators, educators, or leadership coaches in delivering workshops, learning sessions, or guided discussions based on each chapter of *Empowering Strategic Change: Conversation-Focused Project Leadership*. Each set of notes includes learning activities, reflective prompts, and tools that align with the content, purpose, and tools introduced in each chapter.

Chapter 1—Leading by Talking

Learning Focus: Understanding how leadership is enacted through conversation.

Discussion Prompt:

- "When was a time you felt a leader missed the chance to tell the story? What difference might it have made?"
- Reflect on a recent change project. What conversations stood out as helpful or harmful?

Activities:

- Conversation Walkthrough: Invite participants to trace a recent leadership interaction and analyze its impact.
- Group Share: Explore the idea of leadership as conversation, not just direction.
- Leadership Conversation Reflection Worksheet (Tool 1): A guided tool to help leaders examine the tone, timing, and impact of their recent conversations for deeper insight and growth.

Facilitator Tips:

- Emphasize the idea that all leaders are conversation-makers, whether intentionally or not.
- Use short narrative examples to model conversation-as-leadership moments.

Chapter 2—Story as Strategy

Learning Focus: Using story structure to lead through complexity.
Discussion Prompt:

- Why does narrative help people navigate change more effectively than data alone?

Activities:

- Introduce the four-part narrative structure: setting, tension, turning point, resolution.
- Reflection Readiness Scan (Tool 2): A quick self-assessment to gauge a leader's openness to reflective practice and conversational learning in dynamic environments.
- Conversation Reflection Compass (Tool 3): A framework that orients leaders toward intentional dialogue by mapping awareness across four reflective dimensions: self, others, system, and purpose.
- Contrast Exercise: Provide two versions of a project update, one with narrative structure, one without. Ask participants to compare.

Facilitator Tips:

- Model a short leadership story that follows the structure.
- Invite participants to create their own "change narrative in 90 seconds."

Chapter 3—The Five Conversations

Learning Focus: Understanding and identifying key types of leadership dialogue.

Activities:

- Map a recent leadership conversation to one of the five types: Purpose, Commitment, Progress, Resistance, Renewal.

- Role-play scenarios: Pairs or trios rotate through scripted scenarios (e.g., leading a reluctant team, celebrating renewal).

Facilitator Tips:

- Reinforce that these conversations are recurring, not one-time events.
- Use visuals to help participants identify and differentiate the five types.

Chapter 4—Dialogue That Drives Change

Learning Focus: Practicing open, intentional dialogue in complex systems. Activities:

- Practice using open-ended reflective questions drawn from the chapter.
- Conversation Function Audit Template (Tool 4): A diagnostic tool that helps leaders analyze whether their conversations are serving the five core functions, transmission, relationship, sensemaking, alignment, or transformation.

Facilitator Tips:

- Encourage psychological safety. Model vulnerability and curiosity.
- Use Appreciative Inquiry, Sensemaking, or Narrative Reauthoring as microtechniques.

Chapter 5—Narrative in the Project Life Cycle

Learning Focus: Identifying moments for story across project phases. Activities:

- Project Timeline Exercise: Map where story could be used during project milestones (initiation, resistance, midpoint tension, completion).

- Leadership Narrative Playback (Tool 5): A structured reflection practice where teams "replay" the story arc of a project to uncover meaning, emotional shifts, and lessons for forward momentum.
- Dual-Lens Retrospective (Tool 6): Introduce reflective prompts for teams.
- Reflective Storytelling Worksheet (Tool 7): A prompt-based worksheet that helps leaders craft, refine, and share stories that reveal personal insight and reinforce strategic intent.

Discussion:

- How can stories offer both clarity and authenticity during change?
- What narratives currently exist about our projects, and are they helping or hindering?

Facilitator Tips:

- Use a real or fictional project to surface key storytelling touchpoints.

Chapter 6—Storytelling for Alignment

Learning Focus: Using story to build connection between individual work and collective strategy.
Activities:

- Case Study Analysis: Use fictional (or anonymized real) examples of change communications. What worked? What failed? See Appendix F: Case Study Reflection Guide—Leadership Roles in Action.
- Revise a Communication Plan: Using the storyboard method, participants rewrite a confusing project message.
- Metaphor Mapping: Invite teams to describe their change journey with a metaphor ("fog," "bridge," "storm").

Facilitator Tips:

- Help participants see how alignment requires emotional and narrative resonance, not just clarity.

Chapter 7—Becoming a Narrative Leader

Learning Focus: Embedding narrative thinking into leadership identity and practice.
Activities:

- Reflective Journaling and Pair Share: "What leadership story am I living right now?"
- 2-Minute Leadership Moment: Each participant tells a story of a time they led through complexity.
- Conversation Practice Map (Tool 8): Use to audit real conversations for balance of the five functions.
- Narrative Inquiry Reflection Worksheet (Tool 9): A deeper reflective tool that invites leaders to explore the personal, relational, and systemic implications of the stories they tell and live.

Facilitator Tips:

- Encourage vulnerability and self-authorship.
- Introduce Narrative Inquiry prompts for individual and group use.

Closing Activity (Optional):

- Story Discussion: Invite participants to reflect on how their leadership story has evolved throughout the course or workshop.
- "What story do you want your team to tell about your leadership six months from now?"

Appendixes: Ancillary Tools and Resources

Appendix A: Leadership Conversation Reflection Workbook (Tool 1)

To support your journey from the very first chapter, we introduce Tool 1: The Leadership Conversation Reflection Workbook, a foundational resource you'll return to throughout the book. As you deepen your understanding of the Dual-Lens Framework, this workbook becomes increasingly valuable for building reflective leadership habits across different contexts.

Designed to support reflective leadership practice across three key roles—executive leaders, change leaders, and project leaders—each section offers a structured worksheet to guide you through recent or upcoming leadership conversations. It helps you reflect on both the internal experience of the dialogue (Lens 1) and its strategic purpose (Lens 2), reinforcing the practical integration of theory into your daily leadership practice.

Complete each section based on your role or explore all three to deepen your understanding of how leadership conversations shape outcomes, relationships, and organizational change.

Executive Leader—Leadership Conversation Reflection Worksheet

Purpose

This worksheet is designed specifically for executive leaders navigating change, transformation, and leadership conversations. It integrates both the lived experience (phenomenographic lens) and strategic function (conversation purpose) of leadership dialogue.

Part 1: Conversation Overview

What was the purpose of the conversation? Who was involved? What was the organizational context? (e.g., strategy rollout, culture shift, cross-functional alignment) When and where did it take place?

Part 2: Dual-Lens Reflection

Reflect on how you experienced the conversation and the function it served. Consider both perspectives of the Dual-Lens Framework:

From Lens 1 (Experience—Phenomenographic), how did you internally understand or approach the conversation? What assumptions, emotions, or intentions were present for you as a leader?

From Lens 2 (Conversation Function), what was the external strategic purpose of the dialogue? Were you aiming to transmit direction, build trust, make sense of change, align perspectives, or catalyze transformation?

Use this section to explore the connection between how you showed up in the moment and what the conversation was meant to achieve. This awareness can deepen your leadership presence and expand your conversational range.

Part 3: Reflective Prompts

What type of leadership did this conversation require, and what did it reveal about your mindset or habits? Was there a moment when the conversation shifted? What helped or hindered that shift? Which of the five modes did you rely on most? Which felt least natural or underused? If you were to approach this conversation again, what would you do differently?

Part 4: Application and Next Steps

One key insight I'm taking forward. One conversation I need to revisit or reframe. One leadership habit I want to strengthen in upcoming conversations.

Change Leader—Leadership Conversation Reflection Worksheet

Purpose

This worksheet is designed specifically for change leaders navigating change, transformation, and leadership conversations. It integrates both the lived experience (phenomenographic lens) and strategic function (conversation purpose) of leadership dialogue.

Part 1: Conversation Overview

What was the purpose of the conversation? Who was involved? What was the organizational context? (e.g., strategy rollout, culture shift, cross-functional alignment). When and where did it take place?

Part 2: Dual-Lens Reflection

Reflect on how you experienced the conversation and the function it served. Consider both perspectives of the Dual-Lens Framework:

From Lens 1 (Phenomenographic), how did you internally understand or approach the conversation? What assumptions, emotions, or intentions were present for you as a leader?

From Lens 2 (Conversation Function), what was the external strategic purpose of the dialogue? Were you aiming to transmit direction, build trust, make sense of change, align perspectives, or catalyze transformation?

Use this section to explore the connection between how you showed up in the moment and what the conversation was meant to achieve. This awareness can deepen your leadership presence and expand your conversational range.

Part 3: Reflective Prompts

What type of leadership did this conversation require, and what did it reveal about your mindset or habits? Was there a moment when the conversation shifted? What helped or hindered that shift? Which of the five modes did you rely on most? Which felt least natural or underused? If you were to approach this conversation again, what would you do differently?

Part 4: Application and Next Steps

One key insight I'm taking forward. One conversation I need to revisit or reframe. One leadership habit I want to strengthen in upcoming conversations.

Project Leader—Leadership Conversation Reflection Worksheet

Purpose

This worksheet is designed specifically for project leaders navigating change, transformation, and leadership conversations. It integrates both the lived experience (phenomenographic lens) and strategic function (conversation purpose) of leadership dialogue.

Part 1: Conversation Overview

What was the purpose of the conversation? Who was involved? What was the organizational context? (e.g., strategy rollout, culture shift, cross-functional alignment). When and where did it take place?

Part 2: Dual-Lens Reflection

Reflect on how you experienced the conversation and the function it served. Consider both perspectives of the Dual-Lens Framework:

From Lens 1 (Phenomenographic), how did you internally understand or approach the conversation? What assumptions, emotions, or intentions were present for you as a leader?

From Lens 2 (Conversation Function), what was the external strategic purpose of the dialogue? Were you aiming to transmit direction, build trust, make sense of change, align perspectives, or catalyze transformation?

Use this section to explore the connection between how you showed up in the moment and what the conversation was meant to achieve. This awareness can deepen your leadership presence and expand your conversational range.

Part 3: Reflective Prompts

What type of leadership did this conversation require, and what did it reveal about your mindset or habits? Was there a moment when the conversation shifted? What helped or hindered that shift? Which of the five modes did you rely on most? Which felt least natural or underused? If you were to approach this conversation again, what would you do differently?

Part 4: Application and Next Steps

One key insight I'm taking forward. One conversation I need to revisit or reframe. One leadership habit I want to strengthen in upcoming conversations.

Appendix B: The Conversation Reflection Compass (Tool 3)

The **Conversation Reflection Compass** is a practical reflection tool designed to help leaders pause and make sense of high-stakes or emotionally charged conversations. It bridges the leader's **internal experience (Lens 1)** with the **strategic function (Lens 2)** of the dialogue, guiding users through four concise but powerful reflection points.

Ideal for solo reflection, coaching sessions, or team debriefs, the Compass supports both real-time awareness and intentional action. It can be used before or after key conversations, especially during the gray zones of change, to align personal growth with collective impact. The tool encourages leaders to treat every conversation as a learning opportunity by asking:

- How did I show up?
- What was I trying to accomplish?
- What impact did it have?
- What could I adapt next time?

By connecting how conversations are experienced with what they are designed to achieve, the Conversation Reflection Compass strengthens a leader's ability to respond with clarity, empathy, and purpose.

Structure (Compass Points):

The tool is typically organized around four quadrants or "directions," each aligning with a key reflective prompt:

- **North—Purpose:**
  What was the intended function of the conversation? (Lens 2: Transmission, Relationship, Sensemaking, Alignment, Transformation)
- **East—Experience:**
  How did I experience the conversation internally? (Lens 1: Strategic intent, relationship-building, awareness, etc.)
- **South—Impact:**
  What impact did the conversation have on others? Did it create clarity, trust, insight, or momentum?
- **West—Adaptation:**
  What could I do differently next time? What function was missing or underused?

Example—Using the Conversation Reflection Compass

Scenario:
An executive sponsor is addressing cross-functional tensions during a project rollout meeting.

- **North (Purpose):**
  I intended to create Alignment, to clarify roles and reconnect the team to the shared strategy.
- **East (Experience):**
  I noticed I was feeling impatient and focused more on delivering information than creating space for discussion.

- **South (Impact):**
  Some team members seemed disengaged, while others challenged the direction. It didn't land as I hoped.
- **West (Adaptation):**
  Next time, I'll integrate more Relationship and Sensemaking. I'll check in emotionally before jumping into alignment.

Appendix C: Conversation Function Audit Template (Tool 4)

A step-by-step worksheet for reviewing recent conversations to identify their primary function, effectiveness, and alignment with leadership goals.

Date/Context: Insert meeting/project/event

Conversation Summary: Briefly describe what the conversation was about.

Intended Function(s):

Transmission
Relationship
Sensemaking
Alignment
Transformation

Observed Function(s):

Transmission
Relationship
Sensemaking
Alignment
Transformation
What worked well? (Reflection)
What could be improved? (Reflection)

Next Steps or Adjustments: (Plan for the next similar conversation)

Appendix D: Reflective Storytelling Worksheet (Tool 7)

Purpose:
Use this worksheet (Tool 7) to reflect on how narrative practices have surfaced, shaped, or shifted your leadership during a recent project or change initiative. It supports insight across the **Project Leader**, **Change Leader**, and **Executive Leader** lenses.

Section 1: Anchoring the Experience
Project or Initiative Name:
Role Held: Project Leader; Change Leader; Executive Leader; Other.
Timeline/Duration: What was a defining moment for you during this initiative? Describe the moment and why it mattered.

1. What story (or metaphor) best captures your experience?
   E.g., "Turning the ship," "Walking through fog," "Building the bridge while crossing it."

Section 2: Learning Through Narrative
2. What conversations helped you make sense of change, challenge, or uncertainty?
   Who was involved? What did you hear or say?
3. How did your leadership narrative shift throughout this experience? What did you learn about yourself as a leader?

Section 3: Applying the Dual-Lens Framework
4. **Lens 1: Internal Experience**
   ○ What emotions or thoughts surfaced during your key conversations?
   ○ Were there moments of insight, tension, or transformation?
5. **Lens 2: Strategic Function**
   ○ What was the purpose of the conversations you initiated or led? (e.g., alignment, trust-building, transformation, compliance)

6. How can you use narrative more intentionally in future leadership moments?

   Where could storytelling help surface truth, build trust, or catalyze change?

Section 4: Insights to Carry Forward

7. Complete this sentence:

   "The story I will carry forward from this experience is …"

   ○ Optional: Share this reflection with your team or peers. What do their stories confirm or challenge in your own?

Tip for Facilitators:

This worksheet pairs well with a closeout storytelling narrative playback or mid-project narrative checkpoint. Consider printing copies or adapting it to Miro, MURAL, or MS Forms for teamwide engagement.

Appendix E: Framing Our Collective Story—Session Design

Purpose

To foster alignment, build trust, and cocreate meaning around a change initiative, new direction, or team challenge.

Session Structure

1. **Opening: "In the Room Together" (10 minutes)**

   Set the tone with vulnerability and intention.

   Example framing: "Today isn't about presenting answers. It's about listening, learning, and writing this next chapter together."

   Invite a brief moment of check-in: Ask each person to share a word or phrase about how they're feeling coming into the room.

2. **The Icebreaker: "Story Threads" (15 minutes)**

   Everyone writes down one moment in their career where change felt meaningful, or challenging.

   In small groups, they share these stories and highlight common themes.

Goal: Normalize diverse experiences and surface emotional truths beneath resistance.

3. **Building Shared Meaning: "Why It Matters to Me" (30 minutes)**

   Leader shares their personal connection to the change or challenge, what stirred them, what made them uncertain, and what eventually clicked. Invite team members to write a short answer: "What's one part of this change that resonates with me?" "Where do I feel unclear or hesitant?"

   The group reflects on these perspectives without judgment. Use sticky notes or a virtual board to cluster themes.

4. **Cocreation: "Shaping Our Future" (30 minutes)**

   In breakout groups:

   "What does success look like for our team three months from now?"

   "What do we need to feel proud of this transition?"

   Capture ideas visually (e.g., using metaphor drawings, timelines, or storyboards) to make the intangible tangible.

5. **Closing: "The Commitment Narrative Playback" (15 minutes)**

   Each person shares one thing they'll commit to doing or exploring further, framed as contribution, not compliance. The leader closes with gratitude and a reflection on what they heard.

Appendix F: Case Study Reflection Guide—Leadership Roles in Action

1. **Project Leadership (Nia Thompson)**
   - How did Nia use inclusive practices to manage resistance?
   - What governance structures supported psychological safety?
   - As a project leader, how do you balance structure with adaptability?

   Reflection Prompt:
   - When I'm under pressure to deliver, I tend to …
   - What mindset helps me remain people-centered even when outcomes are at stake?

2. **Change Leadership (Marcus Lee)**
   - How did Marcus use story and dialogue to shift mindsets?
   - What helped him surface the emotional undercurrents of change?
   - How do you cocreate the narrative of change with your team?

   Reflection Prompt:
   - Whose voices or stories are missing in my current change work?
   - What narrative do I need to release to move forward with clarity?

3. **Executive Leadership (Elena Patel)**
   - What was significant about Elena's inner shift?
   - How did her transformation influence others?
   - How do senior leaders demonstrate emotional intelligence in practice?

   Reflection Prompt:
   - What kind of presence do I bring to the room as a leader?
   - When I become reactive, how do I recover and realign with my values?

Glossary

adaptability: The capacity to adjust one's approach, decisions, or communication style in response to changing conditions, feedback, or emerging insights.

application: The practical use of concepts, strategies, or skills to achieve desired outcomes in real-world settings.

appreciative inquiry: An approach to change that focuses on identifying and building upon what is working well.

conversational stance: The mindset and orientation a leader brings to a conversation, influencing how they listen, respond, and engage.

Dual-Lens Framework: A model for leadership conversation that combines internal experience (how leaders interpret dialogue) and external function (the strategic purpose of dialogue).

lived experience: The personal, subjective perspective individuals bring based on their unique history, context, and interactions.

narrative capacity: An organization or leader's ability to generate, share, and adapt stories that create meaning and drive engagement.

narrative identity: The way individuals or groups define themselves through the stories they tell about their past, present, and future.

neural coupling: A neurological phenomenon where the brain activity of a listener mirrors that of a storyteller during an engaging narrative.

phenomenography: A qualitative research methodology that studies the different ways people experience or think about a phenomenon.

presence: The quality of a leader's engagement, focus, and authenticity in a given moment, influencing how others perceive and respond to them.

psychological safety: A belief that one can speak up, offer ideas, or admit mistakes without fear of negative consequences.

purposeful action: Intentional steps taken with a clear understanding of the desired outcomes and their alignment to broader goals.

sensemaking: The process of interpreting and understanding complex or ambiguous situations to guide action.

strategic conversations: Conversation designed to achieve specific organizational goals, align stakeholders, and influence direction or change.

References

Åkerlind, Gerlese S. 2025. *Phenomenography in the 21st Century: A Methodology for Investigating Human Experience of the World.* Open Book Publishers.

Argyris, Chris, and Donald A. Schön. 1974. *Theory in Practice: Increasing Professional Effectiveness.* Jossey-Bass.

Berger, Jennifer Garvey. 2019. *Unlocking Leadership Mind Traps: How to Thrive in Complexity.* Stanford Briefs.

Brown, Brené. 2018. *Dare to Lead: Brave Work—Tough Conversations—Whole Hearts.* Random House.

Bushe, Gervase R., and Robert J. Marshak. 2015. *Dialogic Organization Development: The Theory and Practice of Transformational Change.* Berrett-Koehler.

Cowan Sahadath, Kathy. 2010. "Leading Change One Conversation at a Time: A Phenomenographic Study of Senior Leadership Conversations." PhD diss., Fielding Graduate University.

Denning, Stephen. 2020. "The Real Leaders of Agile: Communicating for Understanding." *Strategy and Leadership* 48 (1): 12–18.

Edmondson, Amy C. 2019. *The Fearless Organization: Creating Psychological Safety in the Workplace for Learning, Innovation, and Growth.* Wiley.

Gibbs, Graham. 1988. *Learning by Doing: A Guide to Teaching and Learning Methods.* Oxford Further Education Unit.

Glaser, Judith E. 2016. *Conversational Intelligence: How Great Leaders Build Trust and Get Extraordinary Results.* SelectBooks.

Hasson, Uri, Asif A. Ghazanfar, Brandon Galantucci, Simon Garrod, and Christian Keysers. 2012. "Brain-to-Brain Coupling: A Mechanism for Creating and Sharing a Social World." *Trends in Cognitive Sciences* 16 (2): 114–121.

Humans of Globe. 2024. "Satya Nadella's Transformation of Microsoft." September 2. https://humansofglobe.com/satya-nadellas-transformation-of-microsoft/

Kools, Marco, and Louise George Kearns. 2022. "The Future of Learning and Leadership Dialogue in the Face of Complexity." OECD Education Working Papers, No. 269. OECD Publishing.

McKinsey & Company. 2023. "The State of Organizations 2023: Ten Shifts Transforming Organizations." *McKinsey Quarterly*, April.

Rizvi, I. A., and S. Popli. 2021. "Revisiting Leadership Communication: A Need for Conversation." *Global Business Review* 22 (6): 1–18.

Rock, David. 2008. "SCARF: A Brain-Based Model for Collaborating with and Influencing Others." *NeuroLeadership Journal* 1: 1–9.

Schein, Edgar H. 2013. *Humble Inquiry: The Gentle Art of Asking Instead of Telling*. Berrett-Koehler.

Senge, Peter M. 2006. *The Fifth Discipline: The Art and Practice of the Learning Organization*. Rev. ed. Doubleday/Currency.

Souza, Rodrigo D., and Thomaz Wood Jr. 2022. "The Multiple Lenses of Studying and Approaching Leadership." *Revista de Administração de Empresas* 62 (6): 1–20.

Weick, Karl E. 2001. *Making Sense of the Organization*. Blackwell Publishers.

Zak, Paul J. 2018. "The Neuroscience of High-Trust Organizations." *Consulting Psychology Journal: Practice and Research* 70 (1): 45–58.

About the Author

Dr. Kathy Cowan Sahadath is an accomplished business leader, educator, and author with more than 30 years of experience in strategic project and change management, organizational development, and leadership transformation. She has held senior roles across complex, multistakeholder organizations, leading large-scale change initiatives, building inclusive talent pipelines, and advising executive teams on navigating workforce disruption, digital transformation, and strategic alignment.

Her academic credentials include an undergraduate degree in psychology, an MBA in project management, an MA in human and organizational development, and a PhD in human and organizational systems, where her research focused on how senior leaders use conversation to shape and sustain organizational change. She has also taught extensively in postsecondary institutions, combining adult learning theory, inclusive pedagogy, and outcome-based design to foster reflective leadership and systems thinking across professional and educational settings.

Kathy's ability to integrate practical leadership expertise with academic insight is matched by her commitment to storytelling as a learning and leadership tool. Since 2020, she has written 26 novels exploring themes of entrepreneurship and leadership, identity, resilience, and human connection, stories that resonate deeply with adult learners and reflect the emotional landscape of modern work and life. This narrative lens enriches her ability to design inclusive, human-centered learning experiences and to speak across disciplines and generations.

As a consultant and facilitator, she continues to support organizations and educational institutions in aligning business strategy with organizational change, particularly in areas such as inclusive governance, change communication, and academic innovation. Her writing bridges business practice, research, and creative insight, making her uniquely positioned to contribute to the evolving discourse on leadership, project transformation, and organizational change.

Index

www.ingramcontent.com/pod-product-compliance
Lightning Source LLC
Chambersburg PA
CBHW061317220326
41599CB00026B/4927